The
Elven-Faerie
Spellbook

POCKET EDITION

Published from
The Joshua Free Imprint – JFI Publications
Mardukite Borsippa HQ, San Luis Valley, Colorado
Founding Church of Mardukite Zuism,
Mardukite Academy & Systemology Society
for religious and educational purposes only.

The
Elven Faerie
Spellbook

A DRUID'S BOOK OF CHARMS, SPELLS & ENCHANTMENT

Based on the work by Joshua Free
Edited by Rowen Gardner

THE JOSHUA FREE IMPRINT
JFI PUBLICATIONS

Premiere Pocket Paperback — *September 2023*

Mardukite Druidism (Grade-I, D-Series)

mardukite.com

Reclaim the Magic and Enchantment
of the Faerie World

An official companion volume to the original
"Elvenomicon" or "Elven-Faerie Grimoire"
containing additional lore to add new spark to
any practitioner's craft of Natural Magic.

Open the door to the ancient faerie mysteries!
Now you can easily explore and understand
the physical, magical and spiritual properties
of the Green World of Nature. Invite Nature
Spirits into your life, perform herbal alchemy,
discover secrets of fertility control and more!

Beginners and adepts alike will find that
"The Elven-Faerie Spellbook"
is a handbook worth its weight in gold!

Joshua Free has been paving the way through
the Elven-Faerie glamour of nature magick for
over 25 years, and now presents a follow-up
to portions of the original "Elvenomicon" as a
stand-alone pocket handbook for the first time!

"Elven-Faerie Spellbook" is your key to unlock
magickal charms and enchantments preserved
in the Celtic-Druid and Elven-Faerie traditions.

If you want the best guide possible as your
companion as you get closer to Nature and its
spirits, then "The Elven-Faerie Spellbook" is
the ideal practical manual for you to access
the ancient arts of Celtic Herbal Plant Magic.

Titles in the forthcoming
2023 pocket paperback series
based on the "*Elvenomicon*"
by Joshua Free

Elvenomicon Series-I

The Secret Book of Elven-Faerie

The Elven-Faerie Grimoire

The Enchanted Forest

Elvenomicon Series-II

Secret Legacy of Elves & Faeries

The Elven-Faerie Spellbook

The Book of Ogham

Series titles coming soon
from JFI Publications

TABLET OF CONTENTS

WORDS OF LIGHT

APPENDIX

INTRODUCTION
by Joshua Free

My participation in the legacy behind '*The Elven-Faerie Spellbook*' began during the mid-1990's in the midst of a critical resurgence of 'New Age' interest—and foremost among these popular revivals: the *Celts* and *Druids*.

Elven-Faerie Spellbook is an integral part of a greater body of work pertaining to my personal involvement with *Pheryllt* and *Elven-Faerie* traditions of Druidism for over 25 years. This material was imparted to me by direct personal 'apprenticeship' with its modern developers as reflected in what I've presented as the first <u>*Elvenomicon*</u> series.

The original '*Elvenomicon*' volume contained a trilogy. It first circulated in the underground as "*The Book of Elven-Faerie*," but I later renamed it *Elvenomicon* to avoid confusing the total collection of work with the title of the first discourse it contained: *Book of Elven-Faerie*—retitled *Secret Book of Elven-Faerie* for this present series reissue. It is a separate discourse from the other two parts in the trilogy: *Greenwood Forest Grimoire* and

The Elven-Faerie Grimoire—the first of which is now released as "*The Enchanted Forest*" for its reissue in a series of individual pocket editions. Collectively, this trilogy comprises *Elvenomicon* 'Series-1' and contains my own original presentation of Elven-Faerie Druidic Tradition, now standing for 20 years past.

The subject of 'Faery-Faiths in Celtic Countries' frequently occupies the attention of Druids throughout the ages, but also practitioners of modern Elven-Faerie magical traditions. The influence on 'New Age' revivals of 'Faery Wicca' and 'Celtic Witchcraft' are equally significant. Many customs and 'sabbats' observed today—and quite often taken for granted—very much owe their foundations to the ancient 'Celtic-Faerie Tradition' and what is better known as "*Druidism.*"

"*Elven-Faerie Spellbook*" is the result of many years of experimentation, deliberation and contemplation spent in personal dedication to the Elven Tradition before attempting to set this version of it in down in print. It is a companion work to the former '*Elven-Faerie Grimoire*' in the original series, derived from deep underground sources—ones that have never been revealed by any of its initiates, but which is frequently drawn from by the same—as obvious by compositions of many popular New Age titles that emerged during the 1990's.

The Elven Way and Faerie Tradition are now a part of nearly all relevant 21st century 'new consciousness', 'new thought' or otherwise earth-oriented forms of 'nature mysticism'. My notes that *this* work is based on—as a *"living grimoire"*—have been reevaluated numerous times before developing the present publication. It is often difficult to solidify Elven lore and "words of light" to the printed page—for they are fluidly dynamic, shimmering etherically in the waves of the cosmic sea. This version of a *"spellbook"* has never been published before.

Only "Druidry" and indigenous shamanism reflect the same type of spiritual "pathway" for Human Ascension that is alluded to in Elven Tradition. And if supplemented with our latest spiritual developments for "Systemology," an Elven-Faerie Druid Tradition can be an effective stepping stone on this greater Pathway.

Although most New Age texts equate Elves and other elemental faerie beings exclusively with the Otherworld or Astral Plane, more experienced practitioners understand the connection between these races and a "very real" legacy of Elven-Dragon traditions and the *Tuatha d'Anu* migrating westward across Europe from Mesopotamia and Anatolia, carrying with them a vast tradition and repository of knowledge from the "Ancient Mystery School." These matters are discussed at length in my previous discourse for Series-I, "*Book of Elven-Faerie*" or rather, '*The Secret Book of Elven-Faerie*'.

The term "Elven magic" ("Elven magick") is used to distinguish this "Elven-Ffayrie" system—also called the "*Edaphic Tradition*"—from others in the 'New Age'. However, to the Elves themselves, magic *is* simply "magic" and it comes from an innate faculty—not some "supernatural" facet of life or intellectual study. Once again: Magic is *not* a "supernatural" power. On the contrary, magick is quite "natural" and, in this universe, follows principles of "natural law" or "cosmic law" even if not commonly understood.

When Humans refer to "magick," they are simply referring to an esoteric study and a creative use of forces in the Universe—the same principles that manifest reality on a moment-to-moment basis. It is the practical application of the true knowledge and lore in everyday life. It should always be enacted *towards* one's own Ascension and in acts to manifest a harmonious world for all Life.

True "magick" in the Elven Tradition is innate—they do not require years of arcane study and training that the Wizard Schools of Humans and "Fey-Touched" must resort to. Elven-Ffayrie simply do not see "magick" as something "outside" of themselves. It is developed and refined as part of their everyday natural life—over a period of progressive self-discovery—just as a Human might choose to refine their own personal tastes and skills, affecting muscle memory or some other artificial *automaticity* for experiencing (and creating) reality.

Wisdom of experience—and I mean Self-Honest experiences from a point of true actualized Awareness—develops with time, and this is something that Elven-Ffayrie races are not short on while residing in the 'Lands Beyond'. Elves and faerie folk also view magick as a part of art. When something created or changed becomes charged or imbued with energy as a result of intention, it becomes art—and the Fey learned to use this art to shape the natural world we see all around us as our "reality." And magick—in all of its forms—will create, transform or even destroy some reflection of our global "reality."

"Magickal feats"—as conceived and purported by Humans—are accomplished via the activation of the mind's subconscious faculties—which becomes "potential power." It may be activated with specific use of symbolism and imagery or focal aids that help an individual direct or channel energy.

We are always actively participating in this *game*—but it is only with our *conscious* participation that we have the power to truly and knowingly by creative.

Many customs and methods of raising energy for this very purpose exist—ritual movements, breathing exercises, ceremonial dances—all of which entice the awareness of the total *Self* to become actively involved in bringing about desired results. All intentional acts are "magical"—even when it is cyclic self-talk of defeatism—and we put our awareness and attention-energies into wherever our focus lies.

All acts, whether mundane or esoteric—are magical when they are movements of energy that create change—in accordance with true will—and following natural laws and cosmic principles that may or may not be widely understood. The Human Condition is easily distracted, and so rituals and ceremonial drama; use of music and vocalized intentions; alternative attire and altar dressings; fragrance of sweet and musty incense and flickering firelight—all are effectively used to bring the *Self* into full awareness and control of the *Self* alone.

It is important to realize—especially if you desire a true understanding of "Elven Magick"—that it is not the rituals and incantations themselves that hold the "power" in magic. A catalyst only represents potential until properly used—and that use is based on ability. "Magickal abilities" come from within—first and foremost—from the part of the "individual" that is not "separated" from the All—but is interconnected and linked absolutely to the fundamental Oneness of reality.

"*Elven-Faerie Spellbook*" provides a practical application of Elven-Faerie lore and Druidic magic—as does its companion "*Elven-Faerie Grimoire*"—that has stood the test of time for over two decades and which will continue to inspire aligned realizations of the Elven Way and Faerie Path in perpetuity.

—Joshua Free, Summer Solstice 2023
San Luis Valley, Colorado

THE
ELVEN-FAERIE
TRADITION

a brief introduction to the elven-faerie magical tradition

Elven-Faerie magic is quite different from other occult systems of "magick" that 'New Age' publications propagate. It is dependent on a unique relationship that is maintained between the practitioner and the Cosmos—and is not very concerned with deciphering cryptic formulas or other esoteric ceremonial specifics. As such, it has specific appeal to a certain segment of *Seekers* that find a unique affinity with the "Green World" of Nature, the environment, and of course, the wildlife—plant and animal—residing there.

Unlike other systems of magickal practice, where a magician might enact their craft as an 'outsider' enforcing demands on spirits or enticing them with strange glyphs, the Elven-Faerie Tradition takes the viewpoint that a practitioner shares an innate kinship with Nature, but also the "elemental" world —which encompasses all the spiritual intelligence that is *behind* and *directing* Nature.

In Celtic countries, there are remnants of a true Elven tradition inherent in what they call the "*Fairy-Faith*"—but the reality is that encounters with the spiritual intelligences of the natural world may be found in most all cultures in history, and not exclusively those of Western Europe. In some traditions they are referred to by names or titles that differ greatly from more typical faerie lore. As such, the factual existence of a universal application of Elven-Faerie tradition is still mostly concealed and misunderstood.

In non-Celtic traditions, earthbound nature "angels" are concerned with local affairs on this planet—and were only later treated as "elementals" by mystics and magicians. But at the beginning of present Human civilization, these matters were primarily handled by the 'priests' and 'priestesses' of holy and divine magic. These practitioners maintained a better Cosmic understanding than is generally relayed in common 'New Age' material today. As such, they understood their relationship with the Cosmos on a different level—and from a different perspective—than what is commonly maintained in today's standard-issue consciousness.

Where Humans are concerned, the Fey Folk do not exist without judgment. They favor those that maintain a physical existence in harmony with Nature; and they essentially shun those that are abusive and irreverent in their relationship with the natural world.

By definition, a personal relationship with 'Nature Spirits' is best established and developed *outdoors* in Nature. This contrasts greatly with the cold ritual chambers of ceremonial magicians in other traditions. The Fae are particularly fond of flower gardens and trees, forests and valleys, bodies of water and prairie wildernesses.

It is common for practitioners of the Elven-Faerie Magical Tradition to maintain a personal *'Fairy Garden'* in their yard. This becomes a sacred locale for Elven-Faerie magic—a place where the magician communes with Fairy-Folk and other nature spirits. The method of communication does not always have to be vocalized out loud, unless such feels comfortable and natural to the practitioner. Unlike other forms of 'magick' that often seem "unnatural," Elven magic is brought about by one's own innate nature.

Elemental encounters are more commonly experienced by those that make an active effort to remedy the environmental negligence inherent in the modern world. The type of person that exercises ecological responsibility in their everyday life is quite simply going to find this magic more effective than others. Quite simply, the Fairy Folk and other Elementals are not otherwise interested in assisting Humans—or maintaining a relationship with them—finding them to be a source of great unbalance on Earth.

The Elven Way often demonstrates an understanding of what is otherwise referred to as the "spirit of a place" or locale, meaning the inherent spiritual intelligence that is present, but unseen, in time and space. As a result, we find experiences described where "flower faeries" assist a 'gardener' or the "household brownies" (or gnomes) had assisted someone in 'selling their home'. In essence, these "personalities" are identified as the entities responsible for 'pulling the strings' behind-the-scenes of our reality; and they are only experienced by those that understand the symbiotic and harmonious relationship we maintain with the Cosmos.

The "Fairy-Faith" is called such, not only as a result of a *belief* in Elves and Fairies, but also because of the near-religious level of spiritual practice that synchronously ensues. An individual's "Fairy Garden" has the same associations as an 'altar'—and quite often it is complimented by an assortment of "statues" and "icons" representing Fae.

Perhaps one of the most common 'New Age' experiences with 'Nature Spirits' involves the subject of *healing*—whether physically or spiritually; whether concerning the individual themselves, or some other animal or plant-life in Nature. It is believed that since they live in closer proximity, affinity and harmony to *Life on Earth*, that they not only have a better understanding of it, but also a better working knowledge of how *Life* can operate or be maintained most optimally.

Fairy-Folk are notorious for their relationship with animals—something that is even observed by practitioners of the Faerie Tradition with their own "familiars" or pets. They are particularly protective of, and interactive with, pets and animals—including those kept primarily indoors.

The past several generations witnessed an increased 'psychical' sensitivity in children, and this is a trend that continues today. In truth, the young have always had a better chance at experiencing 'Nature Spirit' encounters just by '*accident*'. It is possible that this is simply because young people were not yet as clouded or distracted by worldly affairs—although this too is changing during the present information-tech age.

There are also many practitioners attracted to the Elven-Faerie traditions because they have an innate sense of kinship with Faerie beings—as if they are descendents of Fae or else that the 'Elementals' (as they are more commonly understood in occult lore) are, in fact, distant ancestors, or even reflections of lifetimes spent in another world, part of another Universe, resembling a *Faeryland*.

All of these are facets of the modern Elven-Faerie tradition as it is observed and practiced today—and as presented within this text in series with the other volumes that correlate with this instruction. May its suggestions and information prove beneficial to progressing your *Crossings into Faerie*.

MARDUKITE MASTER COURSE ACADEMY LECTURE #18[*]

"Danubian Druidism"

Although in the ancient Celestial, Mythological and Pantheistic systems that were derived specifically from the "planets," those traditions, such as in Mesopotamia, are observed as more of a "priestly" practice; with more religious connotations really attached to specific deities.[‡]

Now, when you look at either end of this—whether you move to the East or you move to the West—you see more of an emphasis on "elementalism," and "elemental" patterns. And a lot of that, in the Celtic tradition or in the Western tradition—a lot of associations with that are attached to the origins of Druidism; specifically 'Danubian'—or "Danu-

---

[*] Transcript of a lecture given by Joshua Free on September 23, 2020; revised from "*Druids, Elves & Dragons: Mardukite Master Course Academy Lectures (Volume II)*"—also contained in "*The Complete Mardukite Master Course.*"

[‡] This transcript begins with the lecture already in progress, as did the original audio recording.

bian" Druidism—those primarily connected
to what you've seen as the *"Tuatha D'Anu"* in
the *'Book of Elven-Faerie'*[†] part of *Elvenomicon*.
And *that* is a nomenclature that *I actually* developed. It's ironic to see it now being used
elsewhere to connect "Ancient Druids" with
the "Anunnaki"—but that was something I
actually developed specifically in my works.
And it was not very popular at first.

Unfortunately many still cling on to a very
specific semantic paradigm viewpoint in regards to these studies—these mystical studies, which are supposed to be opening up
one's considerations and freeing individuals
to conceive and perceive of all these different things. Most semantics that we carry,
even to the present day, in regards to ancient history, really pertains to the way it
was documented by some classical writers—
primarily the Greeks and Romans—as op-
posed to how we might understand it from
the actual point-of-view of these individual
cultures themselves.

Even our words "Druid" and "Celt" come

---

† Or the pocket-paperback version for *Elvenomicon Series-I* as *"Secret Book of Elven-Faerie."*

from Greek writings pertaining to European encounters. The Greek writings eventually classify the entire Order and System of the "Druids" based on these encounters; and of which we continue to use today as our classical sources for understanding Druidism.

We find the same thing taking place with our traditional understanding of Mesopotamia. For example, Mesopotamia was never referred to as "Mesopotamia" by the ancient *Mesopotamians.* That's again, a Greek classification term for the region, meaning "Land between two rivers" in the *Greek* language; but not in any Sumerian language. And then, even the concept of "Sumerians" or "Land of Sumer"—the Sumerians, as we know and refer to them, never actually referred to *themselves as* "Sumerians." You see? This is something that's later done by others.

In "Sumerian" language there is no word for "Sumerian." In terms of the language or culture or the "land"—it's always referred to as, for example, the "language" is written *in* Sumerian as, "mother tongue." And then, the land: "mother land" and so forth. It's not classified the way that *others* later accounting for it, or referring to it, from the *outside*, are classifying it. It is *always* these *outside* perspectives that are primarily explored in the pursuit of conventional history.

This is why we deal with things as "*esoteric archaeology*." We don't deal in the "common everyday" version of history—of which has mainly been spoon-fed by those that are really in no better position to define or describe it as the next person. But it's become the common denominator of understanding; common knowledge; the information we assume that all "players" are basically aware of. This common knowledge is really some of the lowest-level information or "postulates" to base a Life and Reality on as you could get. To look any deeper that requires willingness to actually look or face up to these facets of society for what they actually are—and not just for the way they've been presented.

CHILDREN OF THE STARS

As our story goes: we begin with the *Tuatha d'Anu*; or "Children of the Stars" is what is really meant when you look at the semantics behind this. You can trace the vocabulary;

you see references to these beings pop up as either the "White Folk" or "Shinning Ones" or "Light Beings" or "Star Beings." You see this appear throughout many different indigenous mythologies and in the lore behind a lot of different "mysticism" that relates to "ancestral deities" or any of the "Faerie"-type elementals—or any of this type of thing.

These "Children of the Stars," they *arrived* in Keltia—which is what we refer to as all of the "Druidic" or "Celtic" lands in the materials and in the Master Course—and they arrived on Beltane, which is May's Eve. And so we see an emphasis here on a specific point: and this is the origins, of course, of the specifically Celtic observation of May's Eve.

There's other aspects to observing Beltane traditions today—such as those that follow "Great Bear" constellation circle around; and different ways to plot magical timing and calendars—but the significance of Beltane, or *La Baal Teine*, means the "*Fires of Bel*" in Celtic languages. The *Tuatha d'Anu* arrived and apparently, as the story goes, the local air was enshrouded in smoke for three days after they burned their "ships."

They burned their "ships"—whatever they arrived in—just burned them to cinders. This, of course, has begged the question to some: "is that like a *crash landing* of some kind?" or "did they just straight up burn the ships?—some kind of sea-faring ships..." But the references in lore, of course, just saying "ships," and then, of course, being "burned to cinders"—there's obviously no traces or evidence of them thereafter.

When the "Danubians" arrived in the Western Celtic lands, they arrived in Ireland according to ancient texts. And they discover that it is already actually inhabited by essentially a different Faerie race—descendents of "Nemed" or "Fir Bolg"—which means "Men of Bags"—but the Fir-Bolg, as it explains in the *Book of Invasions* (which is an Irish manuscript), they were forced to take shelter as a result of the smoke and fog and everything... They weren't really sure what had actually taken place when the Danubians arrived and basically treated the event as an invasion—a hostile invasion—as recorded in an Irish manuscript called the *Book of Invasions*.

And so you actually have this "war" ensue

between these two "Faerie" races in ancient times; and it's probably not what we would consider "war" today, in terms of activity. But the fact remains that there was already a preexisting society existing in the "Celtic" lands when the Danubians moved through and, kind of, set themselves up as the "higher minds" or "authority" amidst them.

You then start to see a lot of associations—very specific—to "Elemental Magick." Those emerge specifically in relation to lore that's presented in, for example, the *Book of Invasions*. Each of the elements is ascribed these associations. For example, Earth is aligned to "North" and Air is given as "East" and we find many reasons why we can *qualify* this to be the case in later-derived traditions of ritual magick and in regards to Elementalism —but when we're dealing with Druidism specifically and ancient Druidic lore, it concerns the Danubian Druids being represented by *four* "Leaders," each coming from a different "Otherworld Kingdom" in their own rights prior to their emigration to the Celtic lands, and each of them carrying with them a particular "Magical Artifact."

THE "GIFTS" OF "FAEIRE"

And it just so happens the ancient Faerie lore corresponds... For example, the "Cauldron," which is associated with "Water" and associated with the "Western" direction—just so happens to be represented by a figure, the King of the Western Kingdom, which carried the Cauldron—and then a King of the Southern Kingdom, representing Fire, carried the Sword of Nuada. And Lugh, from the Kingdom of Air, carried the Spear, which is the equivalency of the Wand, in the East. And then the sacred Stone, the Stone of Fal—the Sacred Stone of Destiny—on which the Kings were later "crowned" in Ireland, came from a Northern Kingdom, represented by an Earth (elemental) Guardian.

These are referred to in lore as the "Gifts of Faerie." Then, you know, it's just a matter of simple transference to see how an Air Spear from the East becomes the Wand in ceremonial magic and so forth. In reenacting Irish Druidism, a modern practitioner might use these tools, as suggested in the works of Steve Blamires. So, in the north you're setting out a huge stone (for the Stone of Fal);

and you consecrate a large Spear of Lugh and place that in the East and so forth.

So the idea to apply ancient iconic imagery and symbols this way—the concept of applying them to the elements, using them as ritual correspondences and so forth—this is an ancient concept. Of course, we know the ideals of "Magick" and "mysticism"—the "Power of the Self"—and all that, is not restricted to or allocated to any or one ritual tool, but we see these tools take a presence *in* the tradition as it's finally solidified, in terms of "Celtic Druidism" and "Elven Way" and "Faerie Tradition" as a way of reenacting—or of dramatizing—these various ritualistic and ceremonial applications.

In the outline for *Irish Book of Invasions,* I have written here that it "ascribes the origins of Danubian Druidism; that it's linked to the La Tene culture" which is the culture—it's actually described by historians (by) the way it designed its art and pottery styles and some of the ways in which the "spiral patterns" and, kind of, familiar "Celtic" designs can be traced back to the Ancient Near East, based on the use of it, by this "La Tene" culture.

That's what kind of clued me in—particularly the fact that one of the routes that had been taken was called the "Danube River" and I thought, that seems almost too simple, and as it turns out, yeah—it's for sure related to this tribal migration that took place.

The *Book of Invasions* also describes that there were multiple "racial" invasions of the Celtic lands in prehistoric times. And by "prehistoric," we mean prior to history being recorded first-hand in writing. This really can apply—it's not a specific date—it really applies to at any point in a culture where history is not yet being recorded by that culture.

Even after the invention of the mass-duplication of materials and so forth—the manuscripts that we refer to that are the basis of Druidism, like these Irish manuscripts here and so forth—they are making accounts as though they are very ancient knowledge. But even these materials are all mostly less than 500 years old as written materials. Prior to that, we don't really have much recorded because of the enforced over-Christianization and other dogmas that, ever since the Roman Empire, really suppressed the ability to communicate the true "Celtic" tradition.

Prior to that, all of the libraries and storehouses of information and so forth were destroyed by the Romans. I mean, the Romans spent 1000 years actively working to eradicate any traces of Druidic tradition. And then they ended up—their Empire ended up falling themselves. That's how that went down.

But, yeah, multiple racial invasions—the *Nemedians*, which were the "Sons of the Sun"; the *Fomorians*, the "People of the Sea"; the *Fir-Bolg*, which I translate here as "Men of the Dark Earth." And then finally, the "Children of Anu" or the "Children of the Stars." This marks emergence of Danubian Druidism, which is about where we begin to pick things up in terms of our understanding of Druidism: what Druidism represents; the Elements as I mentioned; the ritual tools and so forth. Granted, they have their own lore attached to how these classifications and elemental correspondences have come together; but it's no less effective when we compare it to the other "Elemental" paradigms; they are all working within the same Elemental tradition under various languages.

A concise synthesis of this "backbone-funda-mental-elemental"—the ritual concepts that were all devised from it—the fundamentals can be derived directly from these "*Gifts of Faerie.*"‡ So, we have the *Stone of Fal*, from the Northern city of Falias, coming to us from Morfessa, the High Wizard of the North. This was then set at *Tara*, the "Seat of the Kings" —literally "Dragonkings of Ireland"—and it would scream out whenever a true king had set foot on it.

And this is an integral part of the ancient "Dragon Legacy." The esteem of leadership and sovereignty and what it represented is specifically tied to this legacy—and there is a certain truth inherent in it. We see the same thing with, kind of, our everyday knowledge of "Excalibur"—the whole "Sword in the Stone" motif of Arthurian tradition—that it could only be released from the stone if the "True King" came along, and so forth.

And *that* is actually even related to, and de-rived from, the "*Sword of Nuada*" coming from the city of Finias, carried from the South by Uscias—according to this Mytholo-

---

‡   Often written as "*faeire*" in Elven-Faerie lore.

gy. And yeah, this is the archetypal "Magic Sword"—the Blade, "*Albion*," "*Caliburn*," "*Excalibur*" and such. Of course, it also had the "magical" ability to deal a direct fatal or critical blow with each strike. It was a symbol of the certainty and cutting will—the searing edge of power—directed by the operator.

Thereafter we allocate the Sword or Blade as a symbol of Fire and the South. And then the *Spear of Lugh* is another—also known as the "Spear of Destiny." I should mention that all of these tools are also referred to as the "objects-of-destiny"; so—The Stone of Destiny; The Spear of Destiny; The Sword of Destiny... the concept of Destiny seems to run pretty rampant here.

But the *Spear of Lugh*—according to the lore—emerged from the Eastern city of Gorias and it's carried by Esras. And it's the spear that essentially never missed its target—much as the *Sword (of Nuada)* could be wielded and it would be a critical hit every time—this spear always found its target. So it would, like with a *wand*, direct the flow or attention to the target. It became a symbol of the Element of Air and allocated to East and which again, we can represent with a *Wand*.

And then finally, the *Cauldron of Dagda*—it's also... well, in Celtic Mythology it reappears as "Kerridwen's Cauldron of Rebirth"—and that's directly related to Pheryllt lore. But the legends explain that it came to Ireland by Master Semias, who came from the city of Murias (from) the West and aligned to water.

In one of the legends, the Cauldron acts like a "Horn of Plenty"—it just keeps filling itself with an endless supply of food. Another bit of lore suggests the artifact played a part in "healing rituals," where it could revive and cure the wounded—repair them; you know, you could stick your hand in and it would fix your hand. In later "Arthurian Traditions"—which emerged out of British Welsh Druidism during the Celtic period, or during the Christian period, rather—by that time, the Cauldron motif is connected—via Christianity—with the "Holy Grail" as a life-giving symbol, and the pursuit of the "Grail" as carrying the "Great Mystery" or the "Legacy."

In our present day understanding, there are other connections to the "Dragon Legacy," which is specifically connected to what

you've actually found in some of the "alternative history" and "da Vinci Code"-type
work—"*Holy Blood, Holy Grail*"—and so forth.
You'll find that there's a "Grail Tradition"
also, that emerges, in the Celtic lands, that's
connected directly to Jesus, the Jesus bloodline, the Jesus legacy and so forth.

I've focused on the more basic themes for
our exploration in Grade-I Route-D at the
Academy, particularly for the "Celtic" tradition—then we move into Mesopotamian tradition in Grade-II. But once you explore, for
example, "Druidry" and "Mesopotamia" and
this particular stream as it evolved into the
Western Magical Tradition, it really doesn't
matter from there—if you examine, for example, other forms of Western traditions or
African traditions or Eastern traditions or
other semantics, you will see the common
ground and correlations easily... And even
the Egyptian and the Roman and the Greek
philo... the mythologies and so forth—you
will begin to see certain common parallels.

And these various cultural mythological fig-
ures: although each one is presented within
their own cultural paradigm or point of view

as, pretty much, the *epicenter* of all existence —or the known world—when you take a step back, you'll find that each one of these *epicenters* was actually correlating with all these *other* epicenters; and that they were actually all having, you know, very similar experiences with very similar *"beings"* and phenomenon that all contributed to very similar background stories and so forth.

But each was relayed just a little bit different and specific to the language, the culture, the values, the ideals, and the geographies of different places. A certain mountain would be a home of the God—and if you went 3000 miles in a direction, you'd find another mountain, which was the home of the Gods and was the birthplace of whatever and if you, you know; each one had established their own version of this. And this is—it's not until you really start to see mass migration of human populations that any of this started to be able to be brought together under the banner of a *new* "Mystery School."

Unfortunately, these human populations—as ignorant as they were as they migrated—really just carried with them *their own* values, their own tradition, held on to their own specific paradigms as their stable datum and then, you know, set out to use it to either interpret or invalidate whatever they came along with each step of the way.

But... now, at this point: we're here in the 21st century; and we've got a Master-level understanding that we can access from the Mardukite Academy of Systemology which to work with all this material; and we no longer have to be restricted to any one or another paradigm or semantic-set, when we set out to realize and discover what is actually *true*.

MARDUKITE MASTER COURSE ACADEMY LECTURE #19[*]

"the faerie tradition"

The "Elven Histories" and the History of the Druidry and the Elven Way—the Faerie Faith as it evolved; as it developed—is relayed very succinctly in the *Book of Elven-Faerie*[‡] portion of *Elvenomicon*, or in *Merlyn's Complete Book of Druidism*. It may be explored and relayed in a diversity of ways; it could be connected very easily to studies of the "Dragon Legacy" (as relayed in the *Draconomicon*); it also relates very clearly to Mesopotamia in Grade-II.

When you consider history and cultures and the "mystical" developments from ancient times and then how it later evolved as the religions and traditions carried through the Classical period—what you end up seeing;

---

[*] Transcript of a lecture given by Joshua Free on September 23, 2020; revised from "*Druids, Elves & Dragons: Mardukite Master Course Academy Lectures (Volume II)*"—also contained in "*The Complete Mardukite Master Course*."

[‡] Or the pocket-paperback version for *Elvenomicon Series-I* as "*Secret Book of Elven-Faerie*."

you see this with Mesopotamia and the Anunnaki; you see this with the presence of those same Celestial Deities when they are appearing in other cultures, whether it's the Greeks or the Egyptians; and you see this present even in populations of the "Elven" and "Faerie" and "Dragonfolk" directly, in terms of ancient history—and this all concerns the *Rise of Humans*. As you see a greater rise in the *Human* population, you see, basically, those that are preexisting in "power," kind of bowing out—and setting up other infrastructures and traditions.

Now, in the case of, for example, the Anunnaki in Mesopotamia—I mean this was kind an "archetype" or a "blueprint prototype" area of development. So, you see an institutional "class" step in, where you have Priests and ambassadors and a specific lineage of "Kings" that's all tied to the Anunnaki directly. There's considered a "bloodline" or a "legacy"—a specific "genealogy"—that is carried forth; and you see "Kingship"—you see this in the concept of the "Dragon King," you see this in ancient China, all throughout ancient Mesopotamia, in *Pharaonic* dynasties of Egypt; you see this in any classification or use of "Dragon" iconic imagery to represent "Kingship" and "sovereignty" all throughout Europe.

Of course, this all goes back to a specific programmed association between the "Dragon," "The Land," the ordering of cosmic systems and sovereignty of "Kingship." And so this symbolism gets laid out and we find these specific "beings," which at first are essentially "gods" when you look at the very root of it; the farthest back—the Anunnaki, the Celestial deities—these are considered 'gods'.

And we don't mean "God" with a capital "G" as the 'Origin of All Things'—but their status; their status and their relationship with the Physical Universe. And the status of the ruling power and its representation with the "Divine Right to Rule" is always a mirror of this higher idea. So, it was put into place—it was implanted—in consciousness, that in the absence of these "gods," then we would have specific "Priest-Kings" and a specific lineage of mystics and so forth, you know—might be half-breeds or quarter-breeds or hybrids or however you want to look at that—they were considered a separate class of beings by comparison to the rest of the population.

Now, a lot of this gets related back to physical bloodlines. This of course, begs the question—and a lot of *hoopla* gets brought up about this on the internet—concerning RH-negative blood-types and all this stuff. But, really what is relayed here is just an example or demonstration of various genetic manipulation down through the ages. It led to establishing various 'shadow traditions' and 'underground traditions' allegedly carrying specific lineages of genetic memory that would otherwise be lost, watered-down or diluted through the common population...

And so, these are all important aspects, but when we look at it from a systemological paradigm, to consider, any of these aspects purely from the physical perspective is to be incredibly limiting about our understanding about the Human Condition. And herein lies the beautiful trapping of Grade-I, Route-D. To limit anything to any one or another "genetic vehicle" type, we know to be a falsehood. That only further contributes to fragmentation of a clear and true understanding.

We know that these vehicles, as the Human Condition, are actually capable of an incredible amount, regardless of any of their ancestry. We also know that genetic memory can be systematically resolved for an individual —as far as a separation of that identification with *Self* as a *Spirit*.

We know that *Alpha-Spirits*[†] come in and out of this Universe or Planet all the time. We know that beings have experienced not only countless lifetimes in *this* Physical Universe, but other universes as well, are able to come in and assume points-of-view and command and control over physical action of a "body."

It's when a person is entrapped in that body and identifies *Self* with it that we start to get into trouble. It's only when consideration of "Self" is *for and as* the "body," we start to get into trouble. And so when we refer to these various "Races" and types—well, certainly in ancient times, significant differences existed between various populations and cultures; most of which operated fairly remotely to

† A term used in Systemology to indicate the *Self* or actual "I"or individual as a spiritual being that is independent of any identification with a body.

one another, up until 2500 years ago.

2500 years ago is around the time when the Greeks *first* encountered the Celtic people and Druids and began writing about them in history—about 500-600 B.C. And between then and now, there was *that same amount of* time taking place before that—if you consider the origins of Stonehenge and things of that nature—a couple thousand years *before any* Classical encounters, or the Greeks or Romans or anyone else that encountered prehistoric Celts to write about them for the history that *we* still use today.

And so, anything prior to that in the "Celtic" lands is essentially "prehistory," because it becomes open to archaeological and anthropological consideration and speculation. We can carbon-date various sites all we want, or try to. We make comparison between certain styles of art and pottery that is unearthed, but when it comes to the written records, we actually have to dig much farther and go back to the Ancient Near East and the cuneiform tablets to find records of the type of antiquity that we are often looking to go to— and those begin about *6000* years ago.

There aren't many literary records prior to encounters of the Classical world with the Celts to differentiate or determine a traditional or universally accepted academic history concerning Druids and other "Elven" and "Faerie" traditions; all of the Celtic traditions, all of the "Faerie Faiths"... All of that. And so forth most part—in terms of the "academic world"—most historians have left that area alone.

FAERIE TRADITION & THE NEW THOUGHT.

When we consider that the Spirit is eternal, and that these beings, which would have been intermediaries or descendents of, you know, the "Children of Anu," and descendents of "Priest-Kings" and "Dragon-lineages" and so forth, from very distant times. We would assume that they would, of course, have an increased capacity of ability.

The concepts that later get relayed—in terms of elementals; elemental beings; Elementalism—we know at one point, spiritual entities would have the ability to choose and discard bodies at will; or even be able to inhabit a wider range of existences. For example, you see increased appreciation for "Nature Mysteries" and natural traditions as "Danubian Druidism" goes from being a practice *by* the Elves themselves, the Faerie folk, the Dragon Kings and so forth—and later becomes traditions practiced by a class of Priests or Druids; those that are dispensing a "Human" version of the tradition to the common Celts.

In the beginning, contrary to popular definitions, Druidism is *not* a "religion" practiced by the common Celtic people. Druidism was originally the tradition practiced exclusively by the "highest minds." It was later systematized, codified and then used to establish or organize Celtic society. But, for example, when the "Pheryllt" are present in Wales or the Tuatha d'Anu are showing up in Ireland, we're talking probably 2000 B.C. or so. This is a different point in the evolution of common culture than what is understood today when you just see what it all eventually evolved to.

The idea that there's an Otherworld, or that there's Faerielands and alternate existences, is pretty common to virtually every ancient tradition; as is the idea that an individual decides to be the Spirit of a "Place"—to locate themselves as, for example, a Guardian Spirit of a particular "locale" or even the point-of-view or Beingness of a "Tree" thereafter. These are not ridiculous concepts. We see these elements intermixed between the lines of what is considered "Celtic Faerie Lore" or traditions of the "Faerie Faith" and "Elven Druidism" and so forth.

I mention this because when we deal with Elementals or talk about the Spirits that are inhabiting Nature and consider the amount of time that ancient Druids spent in "communion" with and "communicating" with natural surroundings, it might begin to make a little more sense. And clearly, when the Milesian Celts began showing up and the "Human" populations, races and cultures were starting to all push westward, these ancient beings had the ability to "transition" in to an Otherworldly "Faerie Country"—being driven from their Earthly homesteads.

I traced these prehistoric migrations, for example, based on the patterns of the La Tene culture, based on the way which these individuals set out from the Ancient Near East—whether it was Galatia, like modern-day Turkey or closer to Mesopotamia. But, this evolution showed that as the populations were growing around them, the Faerie were moving farther and farther west themselves; and they had reached the western point around the time of, at least, Stonehenge.

This is why you see a lot of issues with the classification of what is "Druid" versus these "Pre-Druidic"—the Danubians or "Pheryllt" —which we still consider "Druids" and such. And the big argument has always been "well, Stonehenge was there at a time before the Celts were there..." Well, I guess that would be true if you consider that the "Celts" were only encountered and labeled for the first time by the Classical writers in 600 B.C.

Communication and true understanding of history is quite obviously fragmented. There is little dispute about that. Understanding its truth is often a matter that reaches beyond what realizations can be earned from books. It's really a matter of *where* a person is placing their attention that determines what's going to be considered *real* or *acceptable* or within their *reach* of understanding. Because most of the time, their attention has really been diverted everywhere *but this*; and "history" has been treated as such a dry boring subject for a long time.

When individuals start to realize that pursuing any of these esoteric mysteries deeply also means encountering rigorous history lessons—reconsidering all of what has been learned about history; some people become incredibly overwhelmed by that and just sort of put all this "history stuff" aside because it seems like too much to go through.

ELVEN DRUIDISM & SYSTEMOLOGY.

A "Master"—with a Master-level understanding earned at Mardukite Academy—knows that we are treating the "Route of Druidism, Elven-Faerie Tradition and Dragon Legacy" as just the *First Veil*. We consider it part of the *Lunar Level* or *Gate*. We consider it part of the level which has a lot to do with the "magick" and "enchantments" and "glamours" of the various lights and elements and symbolism found in mysticism. To an individual just starting out on the *Pathway*, all of this stuff seems like an incredible new world; it's a "whole thing" when people finally open to that "all of this is there and exists" and "hey, it can be studied without being a devil worshiper—or some other connotation. It is an entire realm in and of itself; its own "continuity"; it's its own "level"—its own Grade or plateau—entrance into it, its own "*Gate.*"

This is really first steps for some people; and to consider that any of this has even taken place in this past on this planet, just thousands of years ago. It's a place to begin. And so this is why this all falls particularly within the domain of Grade-I for the Academy.

And then one particular benefit of Route-D, Druidism or the "Nature paths" is that—in terms of the *Pathway to Self-Honesty*—it does put one in greater contact or communication with the *Fifth Sphere of Existence*, which is "All Life on Earth" or "All Physical Life." This is one step beyond only treating "Human Life" or the point-of-view of the "Human Condition" at the *Fourth Sphere of Existence*. So, it allows someone to begin to operate—or *Be*—or consider point-of-views, or establish lines of communication, with that which is actually "exterior" to strictly a "Human" experience.

That's what is suggested by "shamanism" or "shape-shifting" traditions and such lore—what you see is basically the ability to establish a point-of-view; to establish the center of Beingness *outside* of a consideration of strictly just the "Human Body" or "Human Condition."

So, you have someone that can basically project and command a point-of-view beyond the physical body that they're tied to; the ability to go out and *Be* a "Tree"; to go out and *Be* the "Wolf"; go out and *Be* these other points-of-view, which are points of "Beingness" and points of "Knowingness." And we know that the highest echelon of "Knowing" is "Being"; and *being* something and *knowing* as a result of *that* point-of-view is essentially the highest point of Awareness or understanding that you could have on something.

This is something that we see in the "Nature traditions." Rather than putting an emphasis on just getting along better in the "physical world" and "what rituals can we do to get a better job in this material existence" and, you know, "how to entice the affections of the girl in the neighboring farm" or something like that; this becomes more about an individual 'mystic path' where a Seeker is reaching out and establishing lines of communication with the existence all around us.

And there is no danger behind this pursuit, so long as—like we referred to in previous lectures—that this doesn't become simply a matter of finding more of points agreement with the Physical Universe; or agreeing to facts that the physical and material existence is *all* there is. Fragmentation entraps an individual to this particular point-of-view.

The purpose should always be towards "Ascension." A simple survey of these types of traditions and a simple pass through or just read through with no higher-level comprehension of this stuff, really doesn't get an individual *there*; it doesn't get someone necessarily to these higher points of realization or the ability to understand the concept of *Beingness*, and point-of-views and Awareness— relating it to Nature, natural surroundings, other lifeforms. There's no guarantee that a *passive* or simply a *common* contemporary survey or participation with these "mysteries" is going to get an individual any further.

There we see boundaries—as I've explained—of Grade-I, or the *First Gate*, versus the *Second Gate*. And when we're talking about these "Gates" and "levels" of realization, we're still treating, systematically, the same existence; we're still treating our understanding of universes; we're treating Self; we're treating the concepts of what we can know and what we can do in the directing of energy.

The only difference being exactly what that entails: the parameters and what we're willing to encompass as that understanding—that kind of gets bigger and bigger and we move Awareness up through these 'Spheres' or "Gates" or "Levels"; these points of realization and existence. Because we're moving *up* and this is the point that we start to see this transition—even in the Mardukite Master Course; because pretty soon here, we are encroaching on our Grade-II work.

Grade-II work, for our purposes, *does* centralize on the points and geography in history that is the Ancient Near East—Mesopotamia and Babylon—but the principles, the truths behind all this, as I've tried to explain prior: that which makes any of things effective, and that which has given any of them the ring of truth, carries forth as we move forward—we're able to bring that with us. It isn't a matter of "Oh, well, we spent all this time doing this and that's *all* now nonsense." That really only becomes the case when a person gets *stuck* on a particular level. The actual passing through of this knowledge—the moving through of all the Master Course materials—can actually be done quite swiftly and with total comprehension, so long as a person doesn't get too exclusively immersed, or stuck or hung up on any one of the points.

You're, of course, entitled to your own opinions and to discover what works for you and what works best for the Seekers you instruct —but its important that we have this standard of delivery for the Academy; and that your personal experiences, inclinations and opinions do not affect that standard of delivery when you represent the Academy or this material. We try to eliminate as much of the "reactive programming" in our Pilots and Instructors before we just turn them loose on the world.

It's important that I have demonstrated that the Mardukite Master Course is a fixed set of material an individual can access; whatever edition a Seeker uses, the material still falls within the standards and curriculum outlined for this material. This way nobody is getting lost on it and it's really up to you Masters and Instructors—watching the cues of your Seekers that you're working with—to determine the direction and flow of this information; for *you* to have a complete understanding of it; for your to be able to *relay* it as best applied; and to be sure that your personal inclinations and experience aren't getting in the way of the clear transmission and communicated duplication of this material.

THE
ELVEN-FAERIE
SPELLBOOK

the enchantment of the faerie realm

From the perspective of the physical realm or material world—or Earth—(or what is referred to as *Beta Existence* in Mardukite Systemology) there is an intermediary realm between *us* here and a truer, more infinite, "Spiritual" (or *Alpha*) Existence. The intermediary realm is often referred to in Elven Lore as the "Middle Kingdom" (and in Systemology as the "Magic Kingdom"—the residual of a former "Magic Universe"). In the traditional Semitic Kabbalah, it is represented as "*Yesod*" (or elsewhere in esoteric lore of the "Ladder of Lights" as the "Moon") or "Lunar" level of all potential existences—a Universe only thinly veiled from our own.

Intuitive and mystically inclined *Seekers* are frequently relaying experiences where they have gleaned a "sense" of this other realm; or occasionally have caught a "glimpse" of the 'elemental beings' and "Nature Spirits" that sit silently watching—peering out from between the folds of woodland foliage, the mists, or even riding the backs of animals.

There are vast differences in the portrayal of Faerie races throughout history and by various cultures. In one sense, they reflect the deities and heroes of ancient legend; in another, they seem almost 'angelic' or 'etheric'. A *Seeker* might easily compare the way in which we read of the humanoid "Tuatha d'Anu" of ancient Europe in contrast to the nature of the more 'Otherworldly' "Spirits" that do not necessarily inhabit typical human conditions of existence exclusively.

Even among 'New Age' practitioners, only a select few are drawn directly by inclination to immerse in Elven or Faerie traditions. In many cases, humans are not likely to take the ancient "fairy" and "Danubian" lore literally; they view the bulk of this subject as anthropomorphic misunderstandings about natural phenomenon, weather or biology. There is no 'deeper' (or 'higher', depending on your semantic preferences) understanding accessible to these individuals beyond the physical—or perhaps even what *they* consider the "Mind" (which, itself, has been almost completely misunderstood by mystics and scientists alike).

Reflecting the very qualities of 'Nature', the 'magic' of the Elven-Faerie Druid tradition is perhaps more 'subtle' than other esoteric occult practices. Memory of our direct experience with "Nature Spirits" from childhood often fades with time. The beliefs and practices maintained by the Fae themselves (and also the Elven Wizards that follow this tradition as metahumans in a mortal shell) are representative of Cosmic Order and the spiritual unity inherent in all Creation. It is not concerned with learning methods that coerce spirits or enforce some arcane pact by means of "blasting rods" or any such ridiculousness found in 'ceremonial magick'.

Those who are more 'sensitive' (or develop or 'sensitivity') are more easily able to increase their *Awareness* to perceive subtle effects from the spiritual intelligences that surround us on Earth and during our everyday lives. Such a 'belief' does not carry with it a necessity to believe that we are in any way victims or the effects of a myriad of obscure entities. Yet, all mystics and wizards are called such because they are aware of the interplay of existences that results in the visible manifestation we experience.

Interaction with entities occurs in a variety of ways, depending on a practitioner's sensitivity and also their own unique perceptual 'style'. Some individuals experience things more visibly; others, more audibly; or, even through tactile (touch-based) senses. Most practitioners of the Elven-Faerie tradition also intuit a nearly continuous presence of a particular 'Guardian' or 'Guide' from the Faerie realm. Various traditions obviously interpret the nature of this differently—but many of those drawn to these beliefs are likely to already have at least some sense of reality on '*Faerie Spirit Guides*'.

Unlike the manner of goal-implanting "To Survive" inherent in the Human Condition operating within an experience of *this* material existence, the Fae and 'Nature Spirits' operate from the Magic Kingdom existence that emphasizes a goal "To Enjoy." As a result, these beings are attracted to more light hearted and joyful environments and individuals. When 'Guides' notice a *Seeker* getting 'too serious' about the Human game, they may even intervene by playing small pranks; the most common being to 'hide objects', prompting you to be more aware.

There is also phenomenon associated with portals or 'thresholds'—not only those that are outdoors in 'Nature', but also those that are inherently a part of home-construction; such as doorways, windows, closets, hallways, and of course, mirrors. And this says nothing of those 'magical constructs' made by 'New Agers' intentionally to serve the purpose of such a 'portal'—or 'relay point' for communications between *this* existence and the 'Otherworld'. A sensitive individual may get a 'sense' of subtle energetic differences resonant with these 'thresholds'— even when they are not considered 'active'.

Encounters with the 'Faerie Realm' require a special etiquette that is not altogether common among Humans. There is a respect and courtesy involved that is reminiscent of aristocratic "courts" of legend and history. There is also a special etiquette involved in actually 'addressing' the Fae. It is not likely that a magical practitioner will learn the "true-name" (or "real name") of a specific 'entity' or 'nature spirit'. The name that *is* often given to you by these spiritual intelligences is only for the convenience of having something to call them—nothing more.

Common classifications for the Elven-Faerie 'types' or 'races' are included in traditional lore, but they serve the function of magical conveniences for 'Elemental Magick'—they are not strictly accurate of the Otherworld (Magic Universe). What they do reflect is an even more 'solidly condensed' reality that is relatively 'beneath' the Physical Universe that is identified with the experience of the Human Condition. They do not reflect the "Magic Kingdom" from which *this* Universe condensed from, so much as they are perfect infinite expressions of those 'elements' that we *do* find manifest in *this* Universe.

Fractioning of the "Elemental Realms" into four parts is illustrated in the contemporary standard of the *Hebrew* "Kabbalah" that is used in 'ceremonial magic' and 'esoteric orders' such as the Golden Dawn. In that cabalistic model, *this* Universe is represented as the "Kingdom" (or '*malkuth*') at the lowest (most condensed) order of manifestation. The remainder of the 'Tree of Life' is indicative of the progressive or cumulative descent of the '*Spirit*' (*Self*) and the Universe it considers itself to occupy. This is based on Anunnaki lore of the Ancient Near East.

The lowest 'sephiroth' ('station' or 'sphere') of the traditional "Kabbalah" is often depicted as a circle with an "X" dividing it into four parts. Each of these parts or fragments is indicative of an 'Elemental Realm' that is a further condensation of elements in *this* Universe. Therefore, an Air Realm might be conceived of as infinite (or recursive) space or a 'plane' or "wind" extending in all directions; much like what we conceive of for a Water Realm that would consist of *water* in place of "airy space"—but also perceived as extending 'infinitely' in all directions. Since the "Magic Universe" is more 'fluid' (meaning less condensed) than these descriptions, we must conclude that these are extensions of *this* Material/Physical Universe.

The lowest-most 'compartmented' Universe or Realm represented by this model *is* actually the very extension of *this* Universe that will represent the next level of degradation for the '*Spirit*' and its reality considerations; and we mean of course the Earth Realm of 'rock' and 'stone'. If one could imagine that a plane of infinitely recursive solidity could extend as a Universe, then one can see the future for *this* dwindling spiral of existence.

According to lore, spiritual intelligences of Nature are not tied to permanently physical bodies and forms. 'Nature Spirits' use "faerie glamour" to affect the visible appearance of their size and shape when they manifest more concretely in the Physical Universe. As such, there is little value in emphasizing the various ways that Humans have chosen to conveniently classify or categorize their various encounters with the Other; information that is often passed off as genuine magical lore, when in fact it is simply the local vocabulary of one or another culture, communicating about universal phenomenon.

The earliest recorded cultures often associated 'Nature Spirits' with other lore regarding 'angelic beings' and 'Divinity'. However, in the present text—and in regards to the ancient Eurasian Elven-Faerie Druidic tradition—we are referring specifically to those 'spiritual intelligences' inherent in the living systems found on the Earth planet. By the term 'Nature Spirit', we mean specifically those entities found in 'Nature'—or else the 'Green World'—and quite often we also mean those 'Elemental Beings' encountered frequently by ritual-magicians.

inviting nature spirits into your realm

Our existence and reality is multifaceted or manifold; it is composed of many interconnected parts or dynamic systems. The first and most critical step toward inviting these spiritual intelligence into your life and reality *is* the belief and acceptance—or rather, agreement—with that reality. Phenomenon is taking place all around us in the Universe all the time. Our perceptions are, of course, restricted to the degree of awareness or attention that is directed by an individual. We are not referring to 'made up' things in this book that are not there; we are placing our attention—or shinning a light—on a facet of existence that is simply not often explored.

The second step toward inviting the 'Nature Spirits' into your life is to simultaneously make a place for them (metaphorically and physically) while proving your worth as a 'fairy ally' or 'elf friend'. It is often said that "every flower has its fairy; and every tree has its spirit." Humans carrying this know-ingness in their lives are more likely to experience its reality; they are more likely to effectively invite 'Nature Spirits' into their own lives. Consider, for example, how many 'people' there are in the world—and yet if you don't know anything about someone, have any 'affinity' or 'communication' with them, then there is no relationship at all— and their "existence" seems rather inconsequential, no matter how "real" it may be.

When examining the various collections of lore passed down to us, it is quite clear that 'practical' applications generally surround the tending of herbs, flowers, animals and trees. Doing so forms a 'link' or strengthens a 'bond' that allows the interconnectivity of realities or 'realms'. By sharing in the agreement of considerations concerning Elven-Faerie folk, we thereby open our lives to the potential of sharing such a 'reality'.

One way in which a practitioner can bridge this 'reality' is through intentional acts—or what some have referred to as 'magic' in the past. The most common of these include herb and flower gardens, 'fairy-gardens' or other prepared 'natural' areas that are dedicated to the Fae and Faerie traditions.

A "Sunflower Portal" is easily constructed, economically grown and maintained to support a perpetual '*bridge*' between '*realities*'. This is more challenging in dense urban environments—but is preferably on one's own property, where it is readily accessible for use, observation, and of course, watering. As is often taught in 'magical lore', the preparation and maintenance of 'sacred space' is of particular interest to practitioners that seek to initiate 'magical activity' from *this* side of existence.

One might note that the Elven-Faerie folk are known for fashioning their 'dwellings' from the natural terrain—using their magic and patience to intertwine and entangle the growth of wood and plant-life to meet their own domestic needs when they manifest in the Physical Universe. Magicians and wizards believe that this is simply a reflection of their "Otherworld" 'dwelling-places'. In imitation of this activity, a practitioner will often find results by crafting their own version of the 'Enchanted World' that Elementals and Fae have a preexisting affinity for. The "Sunflower Portal" is a perfect example of this duplicative effort or 'magical act'.

The "Sunflower Portal" is one possible version of a 'planned fairy circle'—or rather, a 'planted' one. To accomplish this, a practitioner designates a particular area for sacred space. It is not required to be a large circle, since most of the Elven-Faerie tradition is practiced (or developed) in solitary. It should, however, be large enough to lie down in—so, at the minimum, using your own height as the diameter of the innermost clearing (circle). Sunflower seeds may be planted every few inches around the outer perimeter of the circle—making sure to leave a couple feet clear for an entrance.

According to traditional lore, 'fairy contact' occurs most often in places and times that are designated "thresholds" or "betweens." By this, we generally mean 'transitions' or 'shifts' from one distinct point to another. These generally reflect the personal or internal 'shifts' in "consciousness" that practitioners experience when they effectively pierce the "veil between worlds" that is all a matter of perception and Awareness—and not so much a matter of physical locales. The actual 'Spirit' or 'Self' has never been truly confined to the Physical Universe.

Thresholds or "between-points" appear all throughout esoteric lore. They are the 'magical' times and spaces assigned to various rites and spells across history and cultures. Clearly the ancients observed (or "sensed") heightened mystical—or otherwise "Otherworldly"—activity taking place during such times. It later became evident that the energy—or at least a presence of Awareness—of such periodic states could be most effectively 'tapped' or 'perceived' in systematically aligned "places" specifically "tuned" to resonate or amplify such thresholds.

Although many books claim an expertise on the subject of *"natural magic,"* much of the true enchantment experienced from Elven Magic and the Faerie Tradition results from personal exploration into these mysteries directly. The 'Secrets of Nature' are gleaned only by direct "initiation" into the folds of its mysteries—which are concealed only because we are no longer accustomed to 'look' beyond the surface world of 'Human Games' that we are indoctrinated into. The 'Key' to the 'mysteries' then, is not found in spells of incantation and fancy symbols, but in elevating *how* to 'look' and 'perceive'.

natural magic: the ancient craft of elven wizards

More than anything else, the esoteric arts of Elven-Faerie Tradition are classified as 'natural magic'—meaning that they regard the 'aspects' and 'elements' of Nature, but also that these practices themselves come naturally to the Fae, even innately. Their type of "magick" differs greatly from what is found elsewhere in the 'New Age' concerning 'ceremonial arts' and 'grimoires'. It is born from a 'natural' understanding of 'Nature' and the 'Universe', and an understanding of the true relationship between "Self" and all existence in creation.

As increasing Human populations began to also observe practices of the 'nature spirits' the cultural charms and enchantments that they imitated came to be called 'folk magic'. It does not consist of ornate priestly rites involving a lot of specialized elaborate tools or obscure glyphs. They are the customs of the 'peasant folk' and practices inherited by 'gypsy witch' family lineages.

The types of 'magic' written down in other volumes of this series—such as '*Elven-Faerie Grimoire*' and '*Enchanted Forest*'—are intended to both preserve the styling of a specific tradition and provide a synchronous coherent focus when practiced in a group, or even individually among those 'sharing' in a tradition. But the words themselves—and the ritual gestures, &tc.—are not where the actual 'magic' is to be found. Such aspects are simply meant to systematically orient a practitioner's attention-energies in a specific way. Eventually, this ability to shift in 'Awareness' or 'consciousness' does not require the ritual 'triggers' and ceremonial 'stimuli' that a practitioner is first introduced to during their developmental period. And such a period may extend for the entire lifetime of some individuals.

'Thresholds' and 'Between-points' are one way a practitioner becomes accustomed to observing (or sensing) phenomenon. These include the solstices and equinoxes, phases of the moon, transitional times of night and day—and places where light meets shadow, water meets land, the forest rises up from the plains, and mountains meet sky.

The "simplicity" of *natural magic* reminds us of what 'true magic' *is*. Too often a practitioner becomes overly absorbed in correspondences and dramatic rites—they lose a clear vision on the actual 'magic'.

For as long as 'magic' has been a concept in this world, there has been a general understanding that it constitutes the act of applying *Will* via *Intention*. It is, by nature, "metaphysical" because it introduces something into this Physical Universe that would not otherwise be present. The 'origination' *or* 'Source' of *Intention* is not locally present anywhere in the Universe, because the actual *Self* or '*Spirit*' exists in a state beyond the confines of *this* Universe. Therefore, we are imbuing or 'impinging upon' *this* world when we induce change via the *Will* and *Intention* from *Spirit*. And it is generally only from this heightened or elevated perspective or awareness from *Spirit* that a practitioner is not only able to experience the enchantment present around them, but also be aware of their own participation in a magical life where an individual is in control of their own '*destiny*' and is able to exercise their own self-determinism in all ventures.

Druid magic, the Elven Way and other Faery Traditions all represent this higher understanding of 'magic' and the 'mysteries' of 'Nature'—even if not all of the practitioners that operate under such a 'title' or 'name' have actually achieved the elevated realizations that are embedded within this 'magical work', otherwise called the 'Great Work'.

At a practical—or 'modern'—level of reality, *natural magic* shines light on the remedy for the encompassing sickness that plagues the Human Condition and *our* world. It suggests just how 'out of touch' and 'out of communication' the Human population really is— having lost sight of the interconnectedness of all life and existence in this Universe.

If one chooses to find it, there *is* a 'high magick' inherent in the simple glamours and charms found in Elven-Faerie lore and wizardry. It is not always immediately obvious, except when one realizes that these simple acts are 'intentional acts'—and therefore, 'magical acts'. Efforts to unnecessarily complicate the field of spiritual mysticism and metaphysics often only occur in an absence of true knowingness and experience.

Enacting the arts of 'Elven Wizardry' is only a matter of opening up lines of communication and affinity with the reality of Nature —and living with the awareness of a 'Fairy-Realm' in your day-to-day beliefs and lifestyle. Doing so allows a practitioner to better shift their 'consciousness' (or 'focus' of one's 'attention' and personal energies) to a higher *'meta-state'* than what's conditioned in the "normative" perceptual level of the Human Condition.

Naturally, the Elven-Faerie tradition is not the *only* route by which this is achievable— but, it is the one presently of concern to this text. Even those esoteric traditions that do not appear to emphasize "Nature" and the "Green World" in their practices must still rely on systematic organization of the *Cosmos* in this Physical Universe for their methods and models to operate as a coherent paradigm of ideas and techniques. For example, you tend to still find many elemental and celestial (planetary) alignments in operations of 'ceremonial magick' or the 'high magickal arts'. There are obviously many parallels between our local Universe and the Otherworld or 'Magic Universe'.

natural magic:
tuning into nature

The 'Mysteries of Nature' are no "mystery." Everything is 'hidden in plain sight' as they say—but, of course, one needs only adjust their vision to *see*. What we call "nature" is actually a 'manifestation' of *this* Universe—and as such, everything that we must know about *Life* and the *Universe* is everywhere around us. This includes the lessons that we might learn which yields greater *Self-knowledge*. For as the wise mystics have said: *Seek to understand yourself and you will understand the Universe.*

"Magic" is the application of "Will" as directed by personal "Intention"—aspects of *Self* (or *Spirit*) that originate from a higher plane or level of existence. Technically, it is this power of "Will" that we impress upon this *Universe* that causes any action or manifestation to occur. These operations take place systematically as a relay of communication (or 'energy') from *Self* that ultimately results in the '*emotional energy*' and '*physical efforts*' manifest in this Universe.

The more elaborate rituals and formal rites appear in the companion volume—"*Elven-Faerie Grimoire*." They form the more traditional structure expected from a 'New Age' practice, complete with initiations, consecration of tools and seasonal observations. However, the 'fine tuning' of the "magic" is not inherently present in ceremonial texts themselves. This results only from practice and experiencing true realizations that advance an individual's progression on their spiritual journey. True 'faerie magick' is not dependent on stringent adherence to a ritual text. It is a clear communication of *Will*.

The '*natural magic*' described in this "spellbook" is based on the premise of 'living in the moment' and applying 'presence' and 'intention' to acts and activities—including the more "esoteric" displays. Whether it is the act of placing stones in a certain way or wearing a type of crystal; arrangement of a garden or gathering flowers and herbs; the burning of incense or taking a purification bath in times when emotional clarity is required—all of these things become 'magical acts' when an individual truly and clearly *Self-determines* that they *are* 'magical acts'.

In many ways, *natural magic* and 'folk magic' are synonymous to one another. They both concern 'simple' charms and enchantments in contrast to more technical "kabbalistic" ceremonialism present in renaissance-era "grimoires" and similar variations inspired by them. As such, the more 'basic' or simple magical arts that survived among the "rural folk" traditions are often overlooked by the more elitist and philosophizing 'magicians'. An innate need exists among many Seekers to *find* a more complicated formula or decipher one more 'spirit name' or 'sigil'—and it often becomes the "gambler's fallacy" in which one more 'pull of the handle' *will be* the 'winning' final secret needed, *&tc*.

In *natural magic*, the elements and tools of effective practice are *given* by Nature—and with the power of *intention*, a stick becomes a 'wand', a stone becomes an 'altar', herbs and crystals and incense all resonate the desired frequencies or vibrations... Every thing comes together so long as the operator is fully *aware* and *present* and acting with *Self-determined* 'intention'. The most carefully crafted ritual text is powerless if it includes any aspects that are not understood.

The basic principles on which *natural magic* is based—and on which it is effective—may be embellished or elaborated on as a means of personalization. However, a practitioner should be careful not to make this the emphasis of their work. Various gestures, vocalized incantations and other regalia may be involved when it effectively assists an individual in achieving their 'focus' and 'contacting' a specific shift in 'consciousness'.

As a basic fact, an individual—when operating from '*spirit*'—does not require any additional tools in achieving a desired state. But where we are concerned with an experience of *this* Universe from the 'vantage point' of the Human Condition, some 'assistance' is often helpful for developing preliminary gains and greater certainty in one's *Self*.

'*Nature Spirits*' are the spiritual intelligence embedded in the very physical systems or natural manifestations that a 'magician' or 'wizard' seeks to enact a "change" in when they perform what we consider "magic." It is considered wise, even among magicians, to operate along the clearest path of least effort and resistance when transferring energy or communication of *Will* and *Intention* from our higher spiritual source down into the interactions we exchange and manifest on more tangible, visible, or physical levels. By working alongside the 'Nature Spirits' in a cohesive relationship, the wizard accomplishes their goals in alignment with various agreed-upon 'Laws' and 'Systems' of the *Cosmos*, rather than in opposition to them.

For example: the basic principle behind the "healing magick" found in a variety of texts (for the 'New Age') is the concept of '*transference*'. This means 'displacing' or 'moving' an (undesired) energy from a point where it is interfering to another point where it is not interfering (or else is diluted or transformed). This only effectively operates as a matter of *Self-determined Intention*. Any symbolic representation employed or verbal incantation uttered is only an 'assistant' to a magician achieving this desired focus with all of their *Awareness*. As a *spell*, an organic substance—like a 'fruit'—might be rubbed on a wound or afflicted area as a 'transference tool' (or catalyst), which is then buried in the earth. And if simultaneously vocalizing the intention is helpful, then do so.

The Sunflower Portal is *Self-determined* 'Sacred Space' where you might go to 'recharge' or 'get grounded' as the case may be. This isn't the only place you might lie down flat against the surface of the Earth, but you'll likely feel more comfortable in a familiar space. In this wise, you can imagine or visualize emotional turbulence "falling away" from you and sinking deep into the Earth. Or else, you might simply spend some time in 'meditation' "tuning in" to the rhythms of Nature—the heartbeat of planet Earth. It does not require a lot of ritual hype in order to achieve this centeredness.

natural magic, herbcraft and earth magic

The planet Earth provides all the tools that a magician requires to practice *natural magic*. In many traditions, the Earth is anthropomorphized as the feminine "Mother" to all living things that require this planet for its existence. In some traditions, the Earth is represented—and even named—as a 'Goddess'. In one way or another, *she* is a provider of the *leaf*, *stem* and *bud* that appear in the magical 'rites' and 'spells' of the Fae.

The practice of "herbalism" or "herbcraft" is an inherent part of *Faerie* 'charms' and 'spells'. In fact, flowers, leaves, plants, roots and sticks—as found in Nature, or reared in a personal garden—are the basic tools and ingredients of *natural magic*. Recommendations and ritual texts employ these ingredients based on "magical correspondences" found in ancient Elven-Faerie and Druidic traditions. These were later carried over to modern times by various cultural vocabularies and traditions throughout history.

The practice of *natural magic* requires care and reverence—and ultimately respect for the 'spiritual intelligences' inhabiting the natural world. This is particularly important when '*using*' any part of Nature—which is to say, '*removing*' any part of Nature for personal use, even "magical" uses. This factor is not stressed enough in magic texts and is an underlying factor in many experiences of "failed magic" and sudden bouts of "bad luck" or similar. While 'spirits' of the Green World of Nature may reflect life-giving beauty and whimsical bliss inherent in creation, there is also the darker side of the equation, where the Universe can also seem quite cold and unforgiving at times.

At one's own basic 'spiritual' state—the 'Alpha' state in Systemology—there is no requirement for creation in a Universe. It is only a matter of deciding—or *postulating*—the 'beingness' or '*is*-ness' quality of something for it to exist. Of course, in the Physical Universe—to play the 'game of *Life*' in *this* material existence—there is a certain set of 'ground-rules' or 'natural laws' that we must have 'spiritually' agreed to in order to experience the Human Condition.

One of these Cosmic Laws—at least as we have agreed to for *this* Physical Universe—regards the 'give-and-take' relationship inherent in a 'closed system' such as planet Earth (or even the greater existence of the entire Universe as a whole). Scientists understand this as a the 'conservation of energy', which is a nice thought for their own physical paradigms, but it is not altogether 'spiritually true'. For example, the actually intention and thought that the '*Spirit*' impinges upon a 'body' is not from within this Universe—it comes from *outside* (or *exterior to*) the closed system of material existence.

In our local system—here on planet Earth—we have agreed to a game whereby everything has its 'costs'; that there are 'actions and reactions'; that 'polarity' exists; and, of course, all 'forces' are constantly enacting to 'equalize' existence toward a theoretical 'balance' point that never actually perfectly occurs—but it keeps all things in a state of 'motion', or at least the appearance of such. In recognition of *Cosmic Law,* an Elvish Wizard (or practitioner of the Faerie Tradition) must act as a steward, guardian and caretaker for the realm which they take from.

While most of the elements and ingredients for *natural magic* are, indeed, found in the natural environment, there is one exception: the tool used to '*cut*' or '*remove*' those ingredients from Nature. In most modern traditions of 'magical herbalists', this tool or blade is referred to as a '*boline*'—a white-handled knife used exclusively in cutting plant-life for "magical" purposes. Use of a 'sacred' or 'consecrated' tool simply adds to the 'presence' of *awareness* being provided to the 'physical effort' as a 'magical act'. A wizard '*lives deliberately*'. This is what a 'magician' is really practicing with the 'magical arts', though it is not often realized.

In more 'Druidic-oriented' Elven traditions, it is not uncommon for the '*boline*' to be a crescent-bladed hand-'*sickle*'. Many practitioners prefer to harvest herbs and plants (for dietary and magical purposes) from a personal garden—something that is very much connected to the Faerie tradition. It is by no coincidence that the earliest pagan cultures were primarily 'agricultural' and their very survival was materially dependent on an understanding and relationship with the land.

When handling living plant-life, particular care is taken so as to not needlessly tear or damage the plant—especially if only a part of it is removed so the main plant (or tree) can continue growing. On smaller plants, the *blade* strike should be made as a single sure upward motion. It is removed silently after first asking '*permission*' from the plant and uttering the intention: "*With this strike, may you grow stronger.*" The act is finalized with a statement of "*Thank you.*"

Flowers play a major role in many Faerie Traditions. Practitioners commonly wear fresh flowers in their hair. Wreath-crowns as head-gear is very popular among pagans. The 'magic circle' may be observed in your 'Sunflower Portal'—but when a temporarily 'circle' is made, or when 'casting' a circle for a group, flowers may be scattered along the perimeter (or a 'garland' may be used).

Many details regarding the 'magical use' of *trees* is found elsewhere within this series. An entire volume—"*The Enchtanted Forest*"—is dedicated to such subjects, along with its companion '*Book of Ogham*'. Therefore, such information need not be repeated here.

the faerie magic of herbs and plants

'New Age' material—particularly that which is on the market regarding '*druidry*', '*fairies*' and '*herbalism*'—must be especially careful in its relay of "folk remedies" and "plant lore." During the rise of the "New Thought" movement in the 20th century, several of its pioneers were forced to confront 'legal' ramifications for the "illegal" dispensing of 'medical cures' or 'spiritual healing'. Even to this day, literature and other products distributed in 'New Age' marketplaces are required to carry various disclaimers. Thus, even in the present tome, we are dealing with a collection of archaic "folk lore" that is not meant to steer critical life decisions by a practitioner without consulting other professional sources in addition to our own.

A practitioner of these arts *should* have a well rounded knowledge base in the matters they intend to practice; whether those matters are those pertaining specifically to the 'spirit', or those that are intended to affect well-being by treating the 'physical'.

'*Faerie Magic*'—as it pertains to plants and herbalism—concerns both the physical and 'spiritual' aspects or facets. We find use of particular herbs in connection to rituals of various intentions due to their 'spiritual' or energetic qualities. We also find the type of "folk lore" that regards the type of 'remedies' and 'potions' concocted by the original *alchemists* of ancient times—and distributed by the very first *apothecaries* or *physicians* that predate the modern pharmaceutical industry of our present-day society.

Within the *Faerie Tradition*, practices of magical herbalism—or *herbcraft*—appear most frequently when applying incense, anointing oils (or perfumes) to a ritual working or "*spell*." Additionally, various "folklore" concerns "*charms*" (and suggestions) for carrying specific flowers, leaves and/or herb-filled sachet-pouches as '*amulets*' to ward away a particular type of misfortune. Some very basic herbal magic *formulae* include:

Lunar Meditations (Moon)—frankincense, jasmine, mugwort, sandalwood.

Love and Romance—apple, cinnamon, rose, patchouli, sandalwood.

Peace and Serenity—acacia, bay (laurel), chamomile, sandalwood.

Wealth and Business—allspice, cedar, cloves, dill seed, nutmeg, poppy seed.

Studying and Learning—cinnamon, mugwort, rosemary, vervain, yarrow.

Success and Charisma—benzoin, cinnamon, dragon's blood, fennel, ginger.

Protection and Safety—anise, basil, frankincense, parsley, rosemary, sage, sandalwood, thyme.

In examining just a few of the uses of herbal amulets in "folklore"—consider that during the 1960's, the 'lucky' four-leaved *Clover* (and larger Irish *Shamrock*) were frequently carried by those seeking to "ward away" military service (or in this case, avoid the "*Draft*"). Elsewhere we find lore of *Nettles* being carried to protect against evil and to overcome fear; a wreath of *Mistletoe* is made to ease the pain of childbirth; *Vervain* is carried to escape one's enemies; *Acorns* are worn to remain youthful and vigorous; fishermen carried *Hawthorn* sprigs to ensure success at sea; ...such a list goes on and on.

Herbal incense and 'magical aromatherapy' are common subjects in the 'New Age'. Not surprisingly, many of the more commonly used 'scents' and 'essences' are frequently available even in your local grocery store—although there are varying grades or qualities of incense to be found on the market. Some of the most common include:

Apple—love, happiness, relaxation.

Camphor—psychic power, clearing.

Cinnamon—protection, sexual vigor.

Eucalyptus—healing, purification.

Jasmine—love, sleep/relaxation.

Musk—courage, sexual prowess.

Myrrh—protection, purification.

Patchouli—peace of mind, confidence.

Rose—love, peace, harmony, unity.

Sandalwood—healing, protection.

Use of incense is a long-standing tradition in practically all ancient forms of '*religion*' and '*mysticism*'. It is pre-manufactured for today's market, though a part of the ancient craft included knowledge to make it.

Archaic books and 'grimoires' record some of the more popularly used incense mixture formulae of ancient times—some of them known best as "temple blends" originating in the Ancient Near East. In the 'medieval magic' lore preserved in *"The Sacred Book of Magic of Abramelin the Mage,"* the balm of *Cedar* (or *Aloe*) is mixed with *gum* and *storax.* *"The Key of Solomon"* suggests a blend of many sweet smelling *gums—Aloe, Nutmeg,* and *Musk.* Another famous "temple blend" employs equal parts of *Frankincense, Myrrh* and *Sandalwood*—and, in fact, these three frequently appear in 'ceremonial magic'.

A practitioner of the Elven-Faerie Tradition is likely to know at least one method for making their own incense. The most basic formula is for small blocks or cones, which is made from a 'dough'. You can even work the 'dough' around a thin stick. The charcoal-free recipe-formula calls for: (6 parts) powdered *Cedar, Pine* or *Sandalwood*; (2 parts) powdered *Frankincense, Myrrh* or *Benzoin*; (1 part) ground *Orris Root*; (6 drops) of a fragrant oil; and (4 parts) of some other powdered incense—worked like a baker's 'dough' mixed with *tragacanth gum-glue.*

Amulet Bags—or 'sachets'—are made exactly like 'pouches'; or else, the practitioner may fashion a similar-style 'bag' using a four-inch square swatch of cloth (of an appropriate *color*). Herbs and small items are placed in the center of the square, then its corners are brought together and tied like a pouch. Alternatively, you could weave a drawstring through holes around the outside of a cloth circle.

If following traditional *Elven-Faerie* lore: 3, 6 or 9 different 'herbs' or 'items' are added to a single *Amulet-bag* before it is *consecrated* and *charged* with the "intention" of a practitioner using a formal 'ritual' or 'spell'. To achieve the desired effect, it might then be carried, slept with (under a pillow) or given away—whichever is most appropriate. The following are just a few basic suggestions to include for some common applications:

Protection (*white*)—ash, basil, bay/laurel, dill, fennel, mistletoe, mugwort, periwinkle, rosemary, rowan, saint john's wort, trefoil, vervain.

Healing (*blue*)—cinnamon, eucalyptus, garlic, lavender, myrrh, rosemary, saffron, sage, sandalwood.

Love (*red*)—apple, coriander, dragon's blood, jasmine, lavender, mandrake root, marjoram, rose, rosemary, vervain, yarrow.

Wealth/Prosperity (*green*)—basil, benzoin, cinnamon, clove, dill seed, nutmeg, patchouli, pine, sage.

arts of natural magic: alchemical herbcraft

'Herbal Alchemy' is most certainly found at the heart of ancient proto-Druidic *Pheryllt* and *Elven-Faerie* traditions. It is the primary facet of 'magic' exposed by *Welsh* lore of "Ceridwen's Cauldron"—and it is clear that *Vervain*, *Mistletoe* and *Oak* are among the most sacred of herbs used by the *Druids*, and of course, Ceridwen's "*Elixir of Wisdom.*"

Concoctions, brews, tinctures, 'mead' and other libations are an inherent part of cultural traditions. Recipes for such 'draughts' may also be found in *Elven-Faerie Druid* lore. In fact, the oldest records we have of these ceremonial *draughts* in European tradition relates very specifically to the *Faerie Folk*— the *Sidhe* residing in the hills and mounds. Often the *Elves* would be seen, during the dark half of the year, collecting ingredients.

In one version, referred to as the "*Draught of Oblivion,*" a practitioner smashes up one gallon of *Elder Berries* into three gallons of good clear well or spring water. This is then boiled together for an hour. Then the substance is strained, and three pounds of dark clover honey is added. When it has cooled, but still warm, one ounce of brewer's yeast is stirred in; then it is covered and left to ferment for two weeks. It is skimmed from the top into dark bottles and corked until fermentation ceases. To perfect such an art, some supplemental "brewing" knowledge might be sought by a practitioner from other sources in addition to *this* book series.

Fragments of lore allude to various "*Elixirs of Sight*"—meaning a type of mystical 'Otherworld Sight' or 'Fairy Vision'—that which would allow a practitioner to be sensitive to (or literally. '*view*') "between worlds."

In one *Welsh* version, we read of a Druid's ability to extend their lifespans beyond the normal allotted years—and of course, along with this is supposed to be an increased gift of *prophecy* or the "second sight" as it is often referred to in the European Celtic lands.

European *White Pine* is of the 'Ailim Ogham' energy current, though traditionally it is given in lore as the *Silver Fir*; but there is a hidden 'Ogham' called *pingwyddon*—or *Pine*.

The *Pine* needles are gathered on the 'Sixth Night' of the New Moon. These are made into an elixir by infusing them in hot water; but using water drawn from the deepest wells, which have never seen the light of day. It is ingested once every three days.

* * * * * * *

Elsewhere in occult lore, we find alchemical preparation of a 'psychic condenser' (a 'focal accumulator' or 'catalyst') in the training provided by esteemed magician *Franz Bardon*—and notably introduced to American paganism by *Ed Fitch.* The instructions for the most basic of these is to:

> "Bring two-tenths of a pint of distilled water to a rapid boil. Add two tablespoons of dried chamomile flowers. Remove from the heat and allow to cool, then filter into a clean container. Keep refrigerated for later use."

Another formula is given for a 'Universal Condenser' along with the suggestion that our aforementioned 'elixirs of youth' and 'cauldrons of wisdom' from legend were, in fact, "well-prepared psychic condensers."

The "universal condenser" formula is a list of components—much like what we find in other fragments of spells in legend: *Acacia* leaves, *Cinnamon* flowers, *Peppermint* leaves, *Tobacco* leaves, *Viola-odorata* leaves and *Willow* leaves, all brewed together.

These types of potions or "condensers" are later used as 'magical ingredients' or 'components' in themselves—such as in place of an 'anointing oil' to activate a magical item or artifact, or to be used inside of a 'poppet' or 'golem' intended to represent the 'body' of a "magically created" elementary being.

* * * * * * *

Elemental, chemical and spiritual 'alchemy' are all systematized classifications of knowledge relating to the separation, identification and incorporation of various 'parts' in Nature. These may be 'elemental', 'chemical', 'metallurgic'—or, in *herbcraft*, they are concerned with the various parts of plants. And one might have noticed that many of the herbal formulae given throughout this book—and other sources of magical lore—often indicate whether the *root* or *stem* or *flower* or *leaf* is used as the component.

Philosophically—or elementally—speaking, each part of a donor-plant is aligned to a particular 'energy' *in addition* to whatever 'energy current' the plant represents as a whole.

For example, feminine 'producing' parts of a plant—those that are operate under the domain of *earth* and *moon*—are the parts that are actually *in* the ground-soil and assist to deliver *water* to the remainder of the plant. These include the roots, main stem (or wood) that grows beneath the outer skin (or bark).

Looking at the other pole—of masculine energy—we find those more visible parts of a plant that are exposed to the *sky* and *Sun*: the leaves, flower petals and outer skin (or bark). So each plant (or tree, *&tc.*) carries its own unique attributes or qualities, as a species; then too, we have these correspondences that are alchemically associated with each part. This all contributes to a greater understanding that a practitioner will carry with them while operating *natural magic*. Far more than incantations, it is "high quality certainty" that makes '*magic*' effective.

an elven-faerie celtic druid's herbal grimoire

Anointing Oils—frankincense, jasmine, lavender, lily-of-the-valley, rosemary, vervain.

Banishing—cedar, clove, cypress, elm, fern, mugwort, rue, st. john's wort, vervain, yarrow.

Binding Spells—apple, cypress, dragon's blood, pine, rowan, wormwood.

Black Willow Bark—one of the hormonal-control herbs of male continence used to decrease sexual drive among male Druids, particularly during developmental training.

Catnip—chewed by ancient Celtic warriors to increase their fierceness in battle.

Divination—cinnamon, hazel, laurel (bay), marigold, mugwort, nutmeg, rowan, sandalwood.

Healing Spells—apple, cherry, cinnamon, clove, hazel, lavender, myrrh, peppermint, rowan, sandalwood.

Hops—also known as 'beer-flower'; one of the hormonal-control herbs of male continence used to decrease sexual drive among male Druids, particularly during training.

Juniper—an incense for sacred visions.

Love Spells—apple, birch, catnip, elder, heather, honeysuckle, jasmine, juniper, lavender, marigold, mistletoe, patchouli, vanilla, vervain, wormwood, yarrow.

Marigold—also called 'sun-bride'; like dandelions, may be rubbed on the eye lids to assist in achieving 'Faerie Sight'.

Mistletoe—also called 'all-heal'; a small pinch of this was added to all druidic herbal remedies and formulae.

Moonwash—made from a half-ounce jasmine flower, half-ounce eucalyptus bark, and a half-ounce mugwort herb, soaked in a dark jar of one-quart rubbing alcohol for one week before straining.

Mullein—also called the 'velvet plant' or 'graveyard dirt' in some formulae; used in various types of necromancy and dark magic.

Narcissus—one of the hormonal-control herbs of male continence used to decrease sexual drive among male Druids, particularly during developmental training.

Rue—an anti-magic herb used in defense against the magic of others; also used in general purification rites or exorcisms.

Sunwash—made from a half-ounce chamomile flower, half-ounce cinnamon bark and half-ounce oak leaves, soaked in a dark jar of one-quart rubbing alcohol for one week before straining.

Valerian—a powerful sedative used for restful sleep and lucid dreaming, often in combination with black-willow tree bark; it also appears in some love-spells.

Vervain—also known as the "enchanter's herb"; found in various magical offerings and rites for warding off attacks, spatial purification and acquisition of wealth.

White Pond Lily—One of the hormonal-control herbs of male continence used to decrease sexual drive among male Druids.

Yarrow—also called 'woundwort' or 'milfoil'; an herb of love and unity.

women's wisdom: emmenagogic herbs and fertility[*]

An 'emmenagogue' is a hormone-affecting substance—usually a plant or chemical synthesis of its properties—that affects feminine fertility. It is the basic component of modern-day pharmaceutical birth-control, but its origins extend quite far into history.

The functional purpose of an 'emmenagogue' is to promote menstruation as a means of contraception—either in the earliest stages of a pregnancy, or as a regimen of normal use in order to prevent such. Apothecaries and rural witches possessed this knowledge during the "Dark Ages"—and they provided 'potions' to those 'customers' seeking to maintain control over their own sexuality.

The safest way of administering an 'emmenagogue', or maintaining a regular regimen, is in a "tea" and/or "tincture" form. Many of the herbs are also available as extracts.

---

[*] Paraphrased from "*The Great Magickal Arcanum*" anthology by Joshua Free, first published in 2008.

For example, *Pennyroyal* tea is safe enough to drink—but the "essential oil" form of the herb (on the market) is toxic if ingested. In fact, most "oil" forms are toxic and used only for 'anointing' or for their 'aroma'. A pinch of *Myrrh* is sometimes added to these formulae—but very little should be used, and again, never in 'oil' form. However, this is originally why *Pennyroyal* tea was popular among 'high-society ladies' in the past.

In ancient Roman times, the *Willow*—particularly the leaves of the *White Willow*—were used to help control fertility and regulate feminine hormones later in life. It is natural source of "*estriol*"—which has since been synthesized in 'labs' for similar purposes. The berries of the *Chaste Tree* are found in the same formulae—and are actually named so for their effect. Some 'Native American' recipes include *Blue Cohosh.* In some Wiccan traditions, *Mugwort* is also added.

To begin a regimen, the above ingredients may be brewed together as a "tea" and consumed daily (even multiple times per day) during the period of a menstrual cycle. This will not only assist in alleviating some symptoms of discomfort, but will also begin to allow the body to associate the properties of the herbs with the menstrual cycle. This cycle should also be kept track of on a calendar. The herbal tea regimen may then later be started in preparation for—or prior to—when the cycle is expected to start. It may also help to promote regularity of the cycles, and in some cases shorten the duration of the actual period itself. When fertility is no longer a concern, the same regimen may be used to alleviate some discomfort associated with menopause.

tbe faerie gem*

In addition to the "*Elf-Stones*" (as described elsewhere in this series of books), there are many legendary '*Amulets*'—gems and stones —that appear throughout magical lore. As relayed in the *Celtic Researches* of author Dudley Wright:

It is said that every Druid wore around his neck, encased in gold, what was known as the *anguinum*—or "*Druid's Egg*." Pliny, in his '*Natural History*', gives one account of it:

"There is a kind of 'egg' held in high esteem by the Druids, unnoticed by the Greek writers. It is called the *serpents' egg*... Its virtue is highly extolled for gaining lawsuits and procuring access to kings; and it is worn with so great ostentation that I knew a Roman knight who was slain by the Emperor Claudius for no cause whatsoever except wearing one of these 'eggs' on his breast during the dependence of a lawsuit."

---

*   Paraphrased from "*Draconomicon 2: The Pheryllt Researches*" by Joshua Free; also available in the anthology, "*Merlyn's Complete Book of Pheryllt.*"

The Druids themselves were called *Nadredd*, or snakes (adders) by the Welsh Bards; and there is no doubt that this famous object of Druidic superstition was manufactured. The serpent was a sacred reptile to the Druids. They supposed its spiral coils to represent the eternal existence of the 'All'. This *snake stone* is traditionally associated with Midsummer's Eve.

In Scotland, the 'egg' was known as the Adder's Stone—and it was in great reputation for the foretelling of events and divination, the working of miracles, curing disease and the gaining of lawsuits.

It is suggested in several sources that 'glass beads' were "earned" by Druid apprentices as symbols of achievement when progressing through various levels of learning. They were often hung on a cord as a 'necklace' as symbols of cumulative mastery or true authority over the 'mysteries' of Nature.

* * * * * * *

Another interpretation of the "Faerie Gem" or *Glain Neidr* (*Gleiniau Nadredd*) is that it is manufactured from 'glass'—possibly even transparent enough to "see through"—and thereby *'view'* the Otherworld Faerieland. In any case, the "glass gem no larger than an apple" (referred to in some legends) is directly connected to the 'Motherhood of Avalon'—which is to say the 'Isle of Apples' or 'Isle of Glass' (now Glastonbury).

It has been further suggested by certain scholars, notably Lady Flavia Anderson in *"The Ancient Secret,"* that the original "serpent's eggs" were spheres of clear crystal used to 'light' the Druidic Beltane and Midsummer "need-fires" via focused sunlight— "sacred fires" that could only be naturally 'lit' by the Sun, by friction, or by lightning.

WORDS
OF
LIGHT

some words of light: a celtic elven-faerie tradition dictionary for spells and rituals*

ABRAHOR: (A) The woodland realm of the Forest; the Wood Elves.

ABROREN: (A) Elves of Abrahor, meaning literally of the Forest and woodlands.

AETHYR: Substance of the Astral World; a sub-atomic field, which light travels on.

AFTERLITHE: July

AFTERYULE: January

AICME: (G) A set of five Ogham letters. There are four in the original system.

AINE: (G) The Queen of Faerie

AIRE: (Q) Holy or divine.

AIRBE DRUAD: (G) A mystical force field, esp. an impassable barrier or hedge.

AISILING: (G) A mystic vision or dream.

AIYA: (Q) Holy One, not in reference to God.

AKASHA: Fifth Element; spiritual fire; union of all Elements; quintessence at the core of

---

* Extracted from the original "*Book of Elven-Faerie*" as compiled from 'ritual texts' contained in "*Elven-Faerie Grimoire*" and other titles in this series.

all existence.

ALARDAN: (M) A festival or gathering of Elven-Ffayrie.

ALB: A prefix or root often referring to Elves; literally "Light."

ALBAN ARTHUAN: (G) Yule or Winter Solstice.

ALBAN EILER: (G) The Spring Equinox

ALBAN ELVED: (G) The Autumn Equinox

ALBANIA: "Land of Elves"

ALBAN HERUIN: (G) The Summer Solstice

ALBANY: "Land of Elves"

ALBION: "Land of Elves"

ALBREDA: (G) Wisdom of the Elves

ALDARON: (Q) Lord or spirit of the trees and forest.

ALDEA: (Q) Treeday, Trewsday or Tuesday.

ALFERIC: (SY) That which is Elvish Magick or Druidic Forest Magick.

ALFI: (G) Elf Power

ALFRED: (G) also *alfredo*; white or Elf-wise, meaning both counsel and a council.

ALGER: (G) Spear

ALTA: (Q) A brightness, bright light or light.

ALURED: (G) Elven council or court.

ALVA: Lugh's sister-in-law in Celtic Mythology.

ALVAR: (G) An army of Elves.

AMA: (SH) Blood

ANAIL: (G) Breath

ANAR: (Q) Sun

ANDUNE: (Q) West

ANG: (SY) The element and metal of Iron.

ANGA: (Q) The element and metal of Iron.

ANNUN: (SY) West

AOIFE: (G) The Queen of Faerie

ARDA: (Q) A plane or region.

ARTH: (S) A plane or region.

ARVA: (A) Flames, esp. the energy current of the Fire Element.

ASHA: (SH) Spirit or soul.

AUBREY: (G) Elf King

AURE: (Q) Daylight or sunlight.

AVERY: (G) Elf King

BA'ISTEACH: (G) Rain, esp. the energy current of the Water Element.

BAK'YAH: (A) A magick word used for counter-spells.

BARDD GWEWLL: (G) Specific shade of azure sky blue; dye used for Bardic cloaks.

BEAN-SIDHE: (G) A mourning spirit appearing around the time of one's death.

BLEEDING: Part of *foison*; inside of foodstuff removed, outside looks the same.

BRICHT: (G) Spellcraft or magick requiring a vocal incantation or spoken component.

BROWNIES: Earth Elementals; the Elven-Ffayrie "chefs" of Faerieland.

BWCA: (G) also *bwbachod*, meaning Brownies (earth elemental faerie).

CAERLLEN: (G) Ffayrie-mounds; literally "Ghost Hills" or "Spirit Hills."

CALAN: (S) Daytime or sunlight.

CERMIE: (Q) July

CERTA: (Q) A glyph, character or rune; pl. *Certar*.

CERVETH: (SY) July

CHOR'N: (A) A dark or black auric energy, esp. putrescence.

CIR: (SY) Circle or ring, esp. a stone circle.

CLOCH: (G) Stone

COIMIMEADH: (G) A Co-walker or Elemental being who appears to be Human.

COIRC: (G) A sacred vessel, esp. the ceremonial cauldron.

COOMLEAN: (G) An Elvensteed or horse.

COOSHIE: (G) An Elven Hound or familiar.

COR: (SY) Circle or ring, esp. a stone circle.

COR ANAR: (Q) The Solar Wheel of the Year

COROLLAIRE: (Q) Ffayrie-hill or "*howe*," literally "green-mound."

CRANNCHUR: (G) The divinatory art of casting sticks, esp. Ogham.

DAETENIN: (A) Dark or unseelie, esp. dragons or dragon-like elementals.

DAEVAUN: (A) Woodlands or forest.

DAN: (SH) South

DEEA CANAYEN: (F) Calendar

DELPHINE: (T) "Elven" [usually feminine]

DESH-IRIAL: (T) Sister [proper]

DESH-KETAI: (T) Father [proper]

DESH-MIEVE: (T) Mother [proper]

DESH-MIRIAI: (T) Guardian of the Home

DESH-NERAIN: (T) Brother [proper]

DESHTAI: (A) To be honorable in following one's destiny.

DES'TAI: (TU) To be honorable in following one's destiny.

DEVIR: (A) To divert from the right path or follow the wrong destiny.

DICETIA: (G) A charm or spell.

-DOR: (Q) Suffix indicating a world or plane.

DORAI: (TU) Loyalty and duty felt towards loved-ones.

DRAKYR: (A) Dragon

DRAVIDIANS: The Tuatha D'Anu and later Sidhe.

DRYS: (GR) An Oak Tree, spirit of the tree or

wren (bird).

DUATH: (S) Darkness

DUILE: (G) The Faerie Elements or Spirit of the Elements.

EA: (Q) also I'ria, the Source of All Being and Creation.

EAR: (Q) Sea

EASA'AHAE: (L) Peace

EDAPHIC: (SY) Stewardship lifestyle, tending soil/Earth, esp. Elven/Sylvanus.

EKAHAL: (SH) Elf Wizard

EKAHUA: (SH) A female spiritual adviser or Ffayrie Enchantress.

EKAHUEI: (SH) A male spiritual adviser or Elf Wizard.

EL: (A) Prefix or root indicating Elf or star.

ELA: (SH) Stars

ELAITH: (A) The spirit of a being or Star-Essence.

ELAITH TOR: (A) "Tower of Spirit"; auric-chakra personal energetic life system.

ELAN: (A) An Elf, literally Child of the Stars.

ELANDRA: (A) Elven

ELAYNOR: (A) also *elynor* and *elinor*, literally Star Dragon.

ELEN: (TU) Elf-Star or Elf-Friend.

ELENARI: (TU) Elf-Friend or Saturday.

ELENYA: (Q) Saturn-day or Saturday.

ELESSAR: (Q) Elf Stone

ELF-DAY: Tuesday

ELF LEAF: Rosemary (or sometimes Elm)

ELFRIDA: (G) Elf Power

ELFSHOT: In reference to when a mortal is struck by an Elf Arrow.

ELGAR: (G) Noble Elf, High Elf, or Danubian Sidhe.

ELIA: (A) The spirit or soul of a being.

ELM: Tree of Elves

ELOR'EL: (A) Moon

ELOYA: (A) Star-Heart

ELPHAME: Elfland, literally Protected-by-Elves.

ELVEN HISTORIANS: see remembrancers.

ELVEN HOLOCAUST: The Dark Ages, a period from 751 AD-1736 AD.

ELVIN: (G) Elf-born or Elf-Friend.

ELVIRA: (G) Elf-Friend

ELWIN: (G) Elf-Friend

ENDOR: (Q) The Middle Earth world of Humans or Physical Plane.

ENNOR: (SY) Derived from endor, meaning world of Humans.

-ENYA: (Q) Suffix meaning day or light.

ERA: (T) The Earth, land or Middleworld.

ERLINA: (G) An Elf, Sylph or Ffayrie.

ERU: (Q) The Source of All Being and Creation.

ERUSEN: (Q) Children of the Stars or Tuatha D'Anu.

ESHE: (SH) Elf-Friend

ESTEVAR: (A) Tonight, this night, evening or nighttime.

EVALA: (SH) Cloak

FAERIELIGHT: A folklore name for the Jack-O'-Lantern.

FAERIE RING: A naturally occurring circle or ring of high grass or mushrooms.

FANA: (IT) Goddess of the Woodlands

FANA: (Q) An invisible veil, esp. veil between worlds and dimensions.

FAUNI: (IT) Female equivalent of *silvani*.

FAUNUS: (IT) God of the Woodlands

FAY: (FR) Ffayrie

FEAS: (SE) Love towards a material object, e.g. "I love books."

FELONIA: (A) Sacred

FELN: (SE) Love towards magick and the Elven Way.

FER-DAN: (G) Bardic Druid scouts, messengers and news collectors.

FER-LAOI: (G) Bardic Druid metaphysical

poets and musicians.

FEW: (G) An Ogham runic character

FEWS: (G) Ogham runic characters, plural.

FFERYLLT: (G) *Pheryllt.*

FIDTH: (G) An Ogham runic character.

FIN: (SH) Air Element

FIRIMAR: (Q) Mortal humans

FOISON: (SY) A game where Otherworld beings steal Human food.

FOLLETTI: (IT) Female woodland spirits; Etruscan Kingdom (Northern Italy).

FORELITHE: June

FUTHARK: (SC) The Norse Elven Runic alphabet.

F'YONN: (SY) Rebirth season, spring, literally the "Light Season."

GAEL: (A) Stone or gem.

GAETH: (G) Wind, esp. the energy current of the Wind Element.

GALADHAD: (Q) Trees, plural.

GALDROSTAFFYR: (SC) Using Norse Runes in manners similar to Ogham Magick.

GE'A: (A) also Gaea and Gaia, Spirit of the Earth.

GEIRT COIMITHETH: (G) see just-halver.

GEIS: (G) A mystical restriction or prohibition, ban or taboo.

GILLACHT: (G) Puberty

GLAM DIAN: (G) The most severe Druidic curse: excommunication.

GLAMOUR: A mystical enchantment where the physical nature/reality is altered.

GLAMOURY: An Irish-Celtic revival of Elvish Otherworld Tradition.

GLORA: (SH) Sun

GNOMA: (GR) The genetic family of the Gnomes, Kobold and Dwarves.

GNOME: Guardians of the Earth, Keepers of the Soil, esp. rocks and gems.

GRAIN: (G) Sun

GREENWORLD: The physical world region synchronous with Elemental Realms.

GWAI: (AL) Sky

GWAITH: (Q) Shadow

HAL: (SH) Festival day

HARAD: (SY)

HERMETIC MAGICK: An underground Greco-Egyptian mystical tradition.

HISSIE: (Q) Mist

HITH: (S) Mist

HOLED STONE: also Holey Stone; Druidic Birth Stone or tool of the Earth Element.

HRIVE: (Q) Winter

HWESTA: (Q) Breeze

HYARMEN: (Q) South

IMBAS: (G) Divine inspiration or gnosis; literally "Fire-in-the-Head."

I'RIA: (T) The Source of All Being and Creation

ISH'MAEN: (F) Unseelie Wizard [slur]

ISILYA: (Q) Moon-day or Monday.

ISTAR: (Q) Wizard; pl. *istari*.

JANDA'HAI: (D) Mortal Humans, literally "Round-Ears."

JUST-HALVER: also *Geirt Coimitheth*; a spirit feeding on essence of what one eats.

KALEANAE: (L) Watcher, esp. of the Universe or a plane/dimension.

KALOREN: (A) The bright path or right way.

KANITH: (A) Lunar energies

KEMEN: (Q) Earth Element

KEROTH: (TU) Brother

KH'DEK: (Q) Ice or glass, esp. when used as a magick tool or catalyst.

KIERAN: (TU) Sister

KIRK: (G) from Scottish *Circ*; meaning a sacred sanctuary, esp. a stone circle.

KOBOLD: also kobolda gnoma, the blacksmiths of the Elven-Ffayrie.

KUSANAR: (T) Twilight

KYELA: (SY) Love

LA'AER: (A) Air Element

LAER: (S) Summer

LAIRE: (Q) Summer

LANDS ABOVE: The physical world or world of Humans.

LANDS BENEATH: The Underworld or Otherworld of the Sidhe.

LASSE: (Q) Leaf; pl. *Lassi*.

LAVENDER: Elf Herb

LEOLLYN: (G) The Sun Father, esp. Llew/Lugh of Celtic Mythology.

LES: (G) An herbal medicine bag or "juju pouch" carried by Shamans.

LIA FAIL: (G) Stone of Fate brought to Tara in Ireland from the Otherworld.

LINCHETTO: (IT) Night Elves, a lineage from the Etruscan Kingdom.

LIVEWOOD: *Wizardwood*.

LOR: (A) To shine or shine bright, esp. in relation to knowledge.

LOTESSE: (Q) May

LOTHRON: (S) May

LUMBULE: (Q) Darkness

LUVA: (W) Elvish bow

MACDACHT: (G) Prepubescent childhood

METONIC CYCLE: Great Year, an observable astronomical period of 19 Earth years.

MIDDLE EARTH: The physical world of
  Humans.
MILANA: (T) Forest
MIR: (SY) Jewel
MYHIDR: (AL) A lover who is a Life-Mate
  but not necessarily a Soul-Mate.
NAIDENACHT: (G) Infancy
NAN: (SY) Valley
NARBELETH: (SY) October
NARIE: (Q) June
NARQUELIE: (Q) October
NARWA: (SY) To "remember," as like an
  "awakening."
NARWAIN: (S) January
NARVINYE: (Q) January
NEL: (G) Cloud
NIA: (A) Master
NIEVE: (T) A lover who is not a Life-Mate.
NINASTRE: (T) Master of the Woods, esp.
  Kernunnos or Dagda.
NINUI: (S) February
NISHTAI: (A) Not to walk or follow one's
  destiny.
NISSA: (SC) A Sylph or Sylve, esp. female.
NOLDO: (Q) High Elf or Danubian Sidhe.
NOLE: (Q) Lore, folklore or knowledge.
NORUI: (S) June

O'FORFAMAR: (SY) Leadership

ONLAY: (G) A charm or spell fixed on a home or specific area.

OR'MN: (A) The Surface World, Middle Earth or world of Humans.

ORNE: (Q) Tree

ORTH: (G) A charm or spell.

OSTARA: (G) also Ostre, Ostera and Easter, *Alban Eiler*, Spring Equinox.

PARMA: (Q) Book

PEHLORA: (A) Water

PERIZADA: (G) Ffayrie-born or Fey-touched.

PHERYLLT: (G) A race of pre-Druidic Dragon priest-kings in Keltia.

PIXIE: (G) often defined as female winged sprytes; actually Scottish Pict-Sidhe.

RAELL: (A) Refuse or trash, esp. energy/habits one wishes to be rid of.

QUENDI: (G) The first-born Elves of Aeurope.

QUENYA: (G) The original language of the *Quendi*; depeicted as "(Q)."

RADE: Times of mass transition of the Seelie Court.

RE'AITAI: (G) Star, esp. the energy current of the SkyFire Element.

RECOGNITION: Innate ability for sensitive

Elven-Ffayrie to recognize other ones.

REMEMBRANCERS: Elvish historians and loremasters.

RETHE: (G) March

ROCH: (A) Elven-steed or horse.

ROMEN: (Q) East

SAETH: (SY) Cloak, esp. of invisibility.

SAELR'IR: (A) Spirit of the Forest

SALAMANDER: also *draco salambe*; Elemental Fire-Drakes or fire-elementals.

SALAMBE: (GR) The genetic family of Salamanders and Fire-Drakes.

SALAN: (G) Salt, esp. the energy current of the Earth Element.

SATURDAY: Fey-Day

SEAN-SGEAL: (G) A folktale or faery-tale.

SEELIE COURT: The Blessed Court, esp. Elven-Ffayrie of the Sidhe.

SELEK'TAR: (F) A spiritual advisor, usually female.

SENACHIES: (G) Bards specializing in Ogham, esp. historical scribes/musicians.

SENDACHT: (G) Old age

SHADOWLAND: also Summerland, realm of the ancestral spirits of the past.

SHAMROCK: also *Trefoil* and *Trifolium*; the four-leaved clover.

SHEA: (G) Fey-touched and/or genius/
  brilliant.
SHELTIETH: (T) Unseelie, unblessed or dark
  in polarity.
SHOL: (SY) Elven Breath, like the Dragon's
  Breath, esp. healing energy.
SIANA: (SY) Yes
SIDHE: (G) pronounced "*shee*"; the High
  Elves of the Seelie Court, esp. Danubians.
SIDTH-BHRUACH: Silverwand or
  Ffayriewand, esp. made from the Apple
  Tree.
SIER: (A) Fire Element
SILPHE: (GR) The genetic family of Sylphs
  and Sylves, esp. the Sylvanus Folk.
SILVANI: (IT) also Sylvani, a masculine
  spirit of the woods, esp. an Elf.
SIMULACRA: An imitation or substitute,
  esp. Human shells an Elf spirit resides in.
SLATAN DRUIEACHD: (G) A Druid's staff.
SLAUGHMAITH: (G) The Good People, esp.
  the Sidth or Sidhe.
SOLMATH: (G) February
STEMLINE: The straight or middle line used
  to align Ogham notches.
STONE OF SCONE: Lia Fail or Stone of
  Destiny.

SYLVA: A treatise on trees or Elvish Forest Magick and wood use.

SYNDARIN: also Sinddarin, a Sylvan Language of Wood Elves, used by Tolkein.

SULIME: (Q) March

TAGHAIRM: (G) Necromancy; summoning (talking to) the dead.

TAURE: (SY) also taur, Forest.

TERRESTAI: Everlasting Forest, perhaps a reference to the Universe.

TIR-NAN-OG: (G) A mystic island of perpetual youth; a ref. to the Otherworld.

THUILE: (SY) Spring

TOR: (A) Tower, lookout tree or tree hideout.

TORLO: (A) Intense strength, brilliance or brilliant light.

TORLORNOS: (A) World Tree or Tree of Life.

TOROTH: (A) Strength of the Oak Tree or immovable Oak.

TRANSIGNATION: An Elemental projects their Alpha spirit into a mortal body.

TRANSITION: The movement between world and dimensions.

TREE OF LIFE: also Yggdrasil, the metaphoric World Tree.

TREFOIL: also Trifolium, the Shamrock or

four-leaved clover.

TROSAD: (G) A ceremonial or ritualistic
court for Wizards.

TUAITHBEL: (G) Counterclockwise

TUATHAL: (G) Counterclockwise

TUILE: (Q) Spring

TUESDAY: Elf-Day

UBAID: An ancient Mesopotamian proto-
Sumerian "Anunnaki" dynastic civilization.

UIAL: (SY) Spring

UNDOME: (Q) Twilight

UNDOMIEL: (Q) Elven-star, esp. a seven-
rayed star.

UNICORN: A Creature of Faerie; an icon of
innocence, love and beauty.

URIME: (Q) August

URUI: (S) August

VARDA: Queen of Stars; also Anu and Eru,
literally "Star Mother."

VASTA: (SY) Awaken

VIRESSE: (Q) April

VIRITH: (S) April

WEDMATH: August

WINTERFILTHE: October

WIZARDWOOD: also *livewood*; wood
removed from the tree by an Elf Wizard.

YEATA: (S) Fire Element

YGGDRASIL: (SC) The World Tree, usually the Ash Tree.

Y TYLWYTH TEG: (G) Name of race residing in Celtic *Caerllen* or Ffayrie-mounds.

ZEISATU: (SY) Consciousness or thought-forms.

ZHA: (T) The future or what is to come next.

ZORVAIN: (SY) Mystically charged, esp. with an intention.

[KEY TO ORIGINS: The source of a word is indicated by the letter or letters immediately following each bold entree. They are (A) Abroren; (AL) Alloryne; (D) Drae'sturi; (F) Firefen; (FR) French; (G) Gaelic-Welsh/Celtic; (GR) Greek; (IT) Italian; (L) Lis'tarii; (M) Miaren; (Q) Quenya; (S) Syndarin; (SC) Scandinavian/Norse; (SE) Silver Elves; (SH) Shiri; (SY) Sylvanus Folk; (T) Tyr Tylwyth Teg; and (TU) Tulari.]

APPENDIX

APPENDIX

an introduction to elven-faerie spells

Elven Wizards and Druids create their own unique 'prayers', which others might just as easily call "spells"—and still there are others that refer to it as "creative visualization therapy." Our minds, the *Self* and its interconnection to the All, may be described in various ways, names and traditions. We are most concerned with techniques that do yield results—regardless of various methodologies and semantics applied to the same use of "Cosmic Law" for thousands of years.

"Elven-Faerie Spells" may be created by an individual for any particular need or occasion. Remember: "magick" to Elves is a creative art—one that the Masters take great pride in. In order to "write your own magick," however, you should be acquainted and proficient with traditional rites and the rules of spellcraft.

Additional information is also available in companion volumes of this series: *"Elven-Faerie Spellbook"* and *"The Enchanted Forest."*

A "spell" is a small act or short magickal working performed in a "Circle of Power" in order to bring about a desired result or movement of energy toward a certain direction. This does not necessarily occur immediately; it may take days, weeks, months and even years (in some instances) to manifest—depending on the situation.

Most common uses of "Faerie Spellcraft" include protection, fertility and abundance, prosperity and wealth, and the banishment of negativity and/or warding away of unwanted energy. There are many other uses of magick—such as the ever popular "single use love spell," which is not dealt with in this tradition of magick. According to lore, the most popular days for magical work in the Elven tradition are "Elf Day" or "Tree Day" (*Tuesday*) and "Fey Day" (*Saturday*).

Every day is *magical*. Each of the planet-oriented days of the week represent attributes connected to a "ray" of the "Elven Star"—which allows us to glean the Sevenfold Schema of the original source tradition in the *Ancient Near East*. Note here: there are seven days—thus seven colors, seven notes of music and naturally seven (6+1) points on the "Elven Star" are all correlated within the paradigm of Elven Tradition.

<u>SEVENFOLD SCHEMA (or ELVEN STAR)</u>

<u>Monday</u>: Moonday; blue; "G" note; pearl stone; silver.

<u>Tuesday</u>: Elf Day/Tree Day; red; "C"; ruby; iron.

<u>Wednesday</u>: Woden's Day; orange; "D"; opal; mercury.

<u>Thursday</u>: Thor's Day; indigo; "A"; sapphire; tin.

<u>Friday</u>: Freya's Day; green; "F"; emerald; copper.

<u>Saturday</u>: Fey Day; violet; "B"; onyx; lead.

<u>Sunday</u>: Sun Day; yellow; "E"; diamond; gold.

Herbs sometimes appear in lore as "Elf Amulets." Acorns aid in fertility rites—and those found by moonlight are symbols of prosperity and abundance. Acorns are essentially the fruit and seed of the oak tree and carry a history of traditional use for fertility, love, and protective spells and charms. They should, unless otherwise advised, always be gathered in daylight hours, preferably at noon. Keep your chosen intention for the amulet in the mind while collecting them.

In ceremonial magick, wands made from oak are often capped with a large acorn tip. Cones (pine, &tc.) may also be used for this —making excellent tools of growth magic.

In divination for "love," a couple may each drop an acorn in still water and watch to see how they respond to each other.

In a spell to encourage a friend to initiate a romantic interest, seven acorns are placed on a small square of white cloth and tied up with a red cord or ribbon to form an "amulet bag." After sleeping with it under their pillow for three consecutive nights, it is buried beneath a rose bush and then the person calls out for the other to come. The acorn is also a nut-food or it may be crushed into "oak flour."

Apple-seeds are natural items of love-drawing magic—though also poisonous in large quantities. The common apple tree is actually a hybrid effort—the result of years of crossbreeding to bring us the familiar fruit we know today. The original apple species—the crab apple (*malus hupehensis*)—produces much smaller fruits, resembling cherries. The *Rosaceae* family of apples is shared by over 3,000 different species, including the ash, bay/laurel, cherry, hawthorn, peach and plum trees. In Druid folklore, apple is also associated with *Queris* or *Quert Ogham* and is the traditional wood of love magick.

Most Celtic scholars associate apples with the Isle of Avalon, called *"Emain Ablach,"* which some also interpret as "Isle of Glass." In fact *"Affalon"* may be a mutation of "Appleland"—perhaps an ancient orchard or grove. One famous magical tool in lore—referred to previously—the Celtic shaman's wand, called the *"craebh ciuil"* or "Silver Branch," was fashioned from apple-wood. The fruit is also sacred to Mystics because it bares the image of a pentagram when cut at its midsection, and is particularly significant to the harvest—the festivals of Lughnassadh and the autumn equinox. In ancient times, the harvest traditionally began with a toast of cider. At Yule, apple-wine *"wassail"* is used ceremonially for tree blessing. Apples are found in natural healing remedies for anemia and are good sources of Vitamins A and E, which may assist purifying from toxins and lowering blood pressure.

According to faerie lore, bay leaves ward away the enchantments, spells and glamour of others when placed under the tongue. Pine-cones—when found by moonlight—are symbols of good fortune, health and well-being. Perhaps the most famous herbal 'Elf-Amulet' is the *"trefoil,"* *"trifolium,"* *"shamrock"* or "clover" that is so commonly identified as a symbol of luck—or to ward away warfare. All herbs require cutting or removal from the land, so it is customary to "ask the plant's permission" in order to officiate an understanding that a spiritual intelligence exists within all life. A common incantation of the "magical herbalist" is:

"With this strike may you grow stronger."

"Magical herbalists" have also designated specific herbs that are held particularly sacred in Elven-Ffayrie Magickal Tradition. These include: dandelion root; chamomile; mistletoe; elder flow'r: hops; Irish moss; rosemary; rose-hips; raspberry leaf; mint; mullien; skullcap; and slippery elm bark. These may be used by themselves or in conjunction with each other for attracting the attention of "Otherworldly folk" in ritual as well as mixed with black tea and drank as an infusion. They calming herbs—and they may aid one in attuning to the energies of the "Green World" and "Faerielands."

To protect a home, an Elvish shaman might use sage and fern to clear out negative energy. Personal sigils of protection could be traced on the four outer walls to conjure a "magick shield." One might use the "Elf-Sign" (star) or a protective 'rune', 'Ogham' —even the "Dragon's Eye"—will generally suffice for banishing and warding against "typical" types of unfriendly (or malignant) energy. A traditional Gaelic-Welsh incantation for this purpose is:

> *Cosaint agus beanachtai yn n'Deith do talamh seo. Dibir na ole agus dona.*

Ask the aid of "helpful" Elementals. Decide and fix on a target or energy current (or ray) that you wish to block. Envision a representation of the unwanted energy or current and feel that it is the embodiment of what are you are warding away. See the auric energy projected from it/them as being blocked or shielded—as if encased in a bubble—which dissolves into nothingness as you say:

> *I command you, by the names and letters*
> *of the Most High, to depart in peace!*

Keys to effective spellcraft are: clarity of intention; the ability to raise internal energy and merge it with assisting external ones; visualization of desired goals clearly; and the willpower to properly release energy so summoned from within and without. The keys—in this order—form the fundamental steps taken in all practices of "spellcraft." The following are some additional tips to aid your faerie spell-weaving:

> —Incorporate only tools and items of a "like energy" to that which you wish to connect with. All others are distractions.

—Visualization skills make-or-break your mystical prowess of directing energy with the Mind, according to Cosmic Law.

—Only call forth or summon spirits and energies specific to your purpose; and only those that accelerate your cause.

—Ask the "Universe" (and/or "spirit guides") to assist carrying ("channeling") or directing release of energies via the appropriate channels.

—Do not dwell on a ritual working already performed, or on what the nature of the results will be, for at least three days afterward. This keeps any energy used for that ritual-spell "out there" "working for you" and not contained or restricted to the vicinity of your thoughts locally.

—Most importantly, it is essential that you believe in your abilities. Remember the ancient proverb that: *all intentional Self-determined acts are magical.*

the elven wizardry of healing and protection

Consecrate a "Circle of Power" in a place receiving blessing, protection and/or healing. Set out your ceremonial tools—or representations of the "Gifts of Faeire"—in their correlating directions. Enter the circle from the northeast by procession if there are multiple practitioners. Go to the center of your workspace unless you are working in a group that allows for using "Elemental Stations." Light a white candle and say:

"May there be peace within my being."

Each participant should do the same. You can then proceed to address each of the directions from the center (altar)—or if performed in a group, other participants may be stationed at each Elemental "quarter."

NORTH: *May peace ring out and extend across northern expansions.*

EAST: *May peace ring out in the east and extend across the furthest plains.*

SOUTH: *May peace ring out in the south and extend to the peaks of the tallest mountains.*

WEST: *May peace ring out in the west and extend to the depths of the deepest sea.*

Light more white candles—as well as a blue and a red one if this rite is for "healing." You may even state affirmations as you light them, before continuing with the rite.

NORTH: *May peace, love and harmony extend to every living being and space in the Universe, especially [name of what/who is to be blessed/protected/healed]. Great Bear of the North, I call now on your strength and the wisdom of the Earth Element. Offer your blessing towards me and extend your protective/healing power on [n].*

EAST: *May the purity of the Air Element enrich all work performed here. May the Winds aid me in purifying the energies of [n]. Hawk of the Eastern Dawn, I call now on your agility and the wisdom of the Sky Element. Offer your blessing toward me and extend your protective/healing power towards [n].*

SOUTH: *May the purifying flame purge and annihilate that which is unclean, especially in this place/for [n]. Great Stag of Southern Flame, I call on your virility and the wisdom of the Fire Element. Offer your blessing toward me and extend your protective/healing power towards [n].*

WEST: *May the blessing of the purifying and healing powers of the transforming waters be upon me in the work that I do towards [n]. Wise Salmon of the Western Sea, I call upon thy True Knowledge and the wisdom of the Water Element. Offer your blessing toward me and extend your protective/ healing power towards [n].*

Return to the center of your workspace and recite the "Elvish Wizard's Benediction"—or the "Gorsedd Prayer" of Druidism. You may use a version from some other ceremonial source or the more commonly known one, provided here:

Dyro, Dduw, dy naw erth, deall Ae yn heal gybod; Ae yng n gwybod, gwybod y cyfi-

awn; Ae yng ngwybod y cyfiawn; Eigarn Ac a garu, caru pobhanfod; Ac ym mhob hanfod caru Duw. Duw a phob dai oni.

Grant us O God, thy protection; and in protection, strength; and in strength understanding; and in understanding, perception; and in perception, the perception of righteousness; and in the perception of righteousness, the love of it; and in the love of it, the love of all life; and in the love of all life, the love of God and all goodness.

May the Source of All Being and Creation extend currents/rays to protect/heal this place/person.

Bless the "target" with "saltwater" and "burning incense." A "smudge-stick" of sage, reed or fern might also be used. Bless the "bowl of water" and sprinkle it on the person and around the person, or in each room of the house and around the outside of the property. With the "salt-water," say at each point:

By the Elemental Powers of Earth and Water do I so cleanse and consecrate [n].

With the incense, at each point:

> By the Elemental Powers of Flame and
> Wind do I so purify and bless [n].

Returning to the center of the circle, complete this portion of the rite by saying:

> May there be peace [in this home/at this
> place/with this person]. May it/they absorb the protection/healing channeled to
> this space "now made sacred" [or if at
> the Grove, "most sacred"].

If there is a faerie-shaman or Druid present, they may wish to seek the nature of an ailment of a person—or the energetic disturbance of an area—by communicating with Otherworld "shadows," "spirit guides" or other kind of energy work that allows for astral communication. Supplemental healing and protection spells may be performed here. Once the ceremonial goals are satisfied, thank the powers and extinguish the energies of the "Magick Sphere."

Would

you

like

to

know

more

???

*Discover other volumes in the Elvenomicon
Druid's Pocket Forest Library.*

*Such as
"The Enchanted Forest" and
"Book of Ogham"*

ANUNNAKI BIBLE

The Cuneiform Scriptures

New Standard Zuist Edition

an abridged version of
"The Complete Anunnaki Bible"
edited by Joshua Free
for founding the
Church of Mardukite Zuism
in hardcover and
pocket paperback

THE TABLETS OF DESTINY REVELATION

How Long-Lost Anunnaki Wisdom Can Change the Fate of Humanity

Systemology Liber-One

based on the lectures
by Joshua Free for
Mardukite Academy
in revised hardcover

CLASSICS OF MARDUKITE MESOPOTAMIA
REVISED HARDCOVER 2-VOLUME SET

SUMERIAN RELIGION

Introducing the Anunnaki Gods
of Mesopotamian Neopaganism

Mardukite Liber-50
by Joshua Free

BABYLONIAN MYTH & MAGIC

Spiritual Traditions and Mysticism
in Mesopotamian Anunnaki Religion

Mardukite Liber-51+E
by Joshua Free

MERLYN'S COMPLETE BOOK OF MAGICK

An Occult Treasury of Sorcery, Druidism and Witchcraft

by Joshua Free

Contains:
"Sorcerer's Handbook"
"Druid's Handbook"
and
"Witch's Handbook"

MERLYN'S COMPLETE BOOK OF PHERYLLT

Lost Secrets of the Druidic Tradition

by Joshua Free

Contains:
"The Draconomicon"
and
"Draconomicon Vol. 2:
Pheryllt Researches"

SYSTEMOLOGY BASICS HARDCOVER SET

THE POWER OF ZU

Applying Mardukite Zuism and
Systemology to Everyday Life
Systemology Liber-S1-Z
based on a classic lecture series
by Joshua Free

THE WAY INTO THE FUTURE

A Handbook for the New Human
Systemology Liber-S1-W
collected works mini-anthology
by Joshua Free

CRYSTAL CLEAR

(Handbook for Seekers)

Mardukite Systemology Liber-2B
by Joshua Free

Take control of your destiny
and chart the first steps
toward your own spiritual evolution.
Realize new potentials of the
Human Condition with
a Self-guiding handbook for
Self-Processing toward
Self-Actualization
in Self-Honesty using actual
techniques and training
provided for the coveted
"Mardukite Systemology Grade-III
Self-Defragmentation Course Program"
—once only available
directly and privately from
the underground Systemology Society.

Discover the amazing power behind the
applied spiritual technology
used for counseling and advisement in
the tradition of Mardukite Zuism.

19 95   20 20

JOSHUA FREE

PUBLISHED BY THE **JOSHUA FREE** IMPRINT REPRESENTING

The Mardukite Academy of Systemology

THE JOSHUA FREE IMPRINT
JFI PUBLICATIONS

MARDUKITE
ZUISM

mardukite.com

www.ingramcontent.com/pod-product-compliance
Lightning Source LLC
Chambersburg PA
CBHW011222120626
46545CB00010B/3110